Signs of Contradiction

Signs of Contradiction

RELIGIOUS LIFE
IN A TIME OF CHANGE

by Anselm W. Romb, O.F.M. Conv.

B. HERDER BOOK CO. *St. Louis and London*

NIHIL OBSTAT:
John Chrysostom Szymkowiak, O.F.M.Conv.
Censor deputatus

IMPRIMI POTEST:
Anastasius Kuzdrzal, O.F.M.Conv.
Minister Provincial

IMPRIMATUR:
✠Joseph Cardinal Ritter
Archbishop of St. Louis
November 2, 1966

CONTENTS

1 : Failures in Formation   1

2 : A "Sacramental" View of the Vows   11

3 : Love of the World   22

4 : Up-dating, or Belonging to the Present   34

5 : "By This Shall All Men Know . . ."   46

6 : On Being Human   56

7 : The Service of Love: Authority   68

8 : The Love of Service: Obedience   79

9 : Love: The Base of the Pyramid   91

10 : "Cast Your Care Upon the Lord . . ."   103

11 : "Let Him Take It . . ."   114

12 : Puritanism in Religious Life   123

13 : The Mortification of Atonement   133

14 : The Mortification of the Moment   143

15 : Maturity in Religious Life   151

16 : "Be Not Wise in Your Own Conceit"   161

17 : Spiritual Reading: Profit and Loss   170

18 : Public Prayers and Private Sentiments   180

19 : "We Proclaim the Death of the Lord . . ."   189

20 : The Prayer of Contact   198

21 : By Way of Summary   208

1 : Failures in Formation

HAVE YOU ever seen the launching pad of a rocket at one of the military installations or at least on television? The rocket may be powerful in flight and a glorious result of planning and human ingenuity. Yet long before it thrusts itself upward, it is designed to stand earthbound and poised on its pad. Without props and technical preparation the launching and flight would be fruitless.

The comparison to the novitiate is obvious. The seclusion of these months makes us earthbound, one might say. Technical preparation is the explanation of the vows we profess. The direction in which we are geared is the historical spirit of our community as manifested in its apostolate. A fertile mind will suggest other areas of comparison.

My whole point, however, is that the unseen *groundwork* far outranks the execution of the flight in effort, even though the preparation is not for its own sake, but is ordered and designed—in the novitiate—for God's glory and souls' salvation. It is a fairly safe assumption that all religious were anxious on the day of profession to be a witness to *Christ-life* by interpreting the Gospel for their own time and their own nation. What happened after the launching?

Was the novitiate too regimented? Did clocks regulate them more than conviction? Did the superiors' insistence on religious propriety and the discipline of custom overshadow the spontaneous inspirations of grace? Did emotional uplift and pious stories overlaid with sentiment, but with too little theology and canon law, carry them through and past the novitiate? Did fear of disgrace at home and moral pressure from the family, combined with innate pride over being singled out and respected by others as religious, suppress the urge to leave before committed by *oath* to serve God? Did the fear of hell and the loss of salvation preclude an honest analysis of their ability to keep the vows?

The older manuals notwithstanding, it is unlikely in our times that a candidate stays on because of inability to "face the world" and the desire for a safe refuge in the cloister. No one comes to religious life to "loaf with dignity," even though it may turn out that way for some few. In any event, the props of the novitiate and training periods generally prepare us to live peacefully enough and take orders as *young* religious. But a decade of service, experience in the field, awareness of the superior dedication of some laity, the gripping problem of survival of the poor in comparison with our financial security, the humiliation of others living in depressed areas or with inferior education and without even civil rights as compared with the respect shown us—these are the troubled waters of a mature religious' conscience when he senses the inadequacy of his own Christ-life. I have seen religious and diocesan priests consumed slowly by their own deficiencies and even become alcoholics when they could not meet the challenge of laymen with better education, political acumen, and a flair for leadership. They would be resentful of the lay persons or of the system of which they were the products. There is often a loss of faith in God, besides in oneself, when prayer-life comes to a standstill. These problems of faith need separate treatment later on. Perhaps one part of the faulty system of training in the novitiate was emphasis on manual labor because it was so "wholesome to be tired at the end of the day." Perhaps it was the cursory knowledge of the history and ideals of the community, or a haphazard training in the theological and canonical character of the vows. Both male and female religious have been guilty in this respect.

Surely the materialism of our times can explain why some religious leave a community, as those priest-religious who secularize and others who transfer to the lay state—these latter too often without ecclesiastical permission and dispensations. The *exaggerated* emphasis on democracy, carried over into religious life, may account for others' disaffection. But what shall we say of the defection of older religious men and women who suddenly decide to desert their community—even with ecclesiastical leave, as, for example, when they are no longer appointed or elected superiors? How shall we assess the melancholy indifference of the older religious to the updating current in the Church. The frequency of such a state of affairs underscores the need to *begin* religious life well in the days of training.

It is tiresome, however, to hear the blame placed continually on the "times" in which we live and its secularism. There are dedicated men and women who serve in government and education at less pay than they might receive in business. There are those who even give a year or two of their lives gratis to social service in our nation and abroad as a part of the overseas corps to demonstrate their belief in democracy by living it. The tragedy is that religious communities do not attract and seem to lose so many of the most intelligent and originally most dedicated souls.

Government agencies carry on so much caritative work and grant so much aid, even on the moral plane through counseling techniques, that we religious have to justify ourselves to the world on the grounds of our personal commitment to God. Someone may object that we are not bound to justify ourselves to anyone but God and his representatives. Such an observation only points out the objector's poor grasp of the meaning of a religious vocation—*to relive Christ's life in at least one of its aspects:* to preach, to care for the sick, to instruct, to pray in solitude. We are not, however, living a Christ-life unless it somehow touches others in a vital and compelling way.

Among the more ill-used phrases of Scriptures is the dictum that "this is the will of God, your sanctification." Surely personal sanctification *is* the soul of our apostolate, but only if adequately understood. No one is saved or damned alone, the spiritual writers rightly say. But ignorance of the social ills of one's environment, the political and financial sins of the community and the moral turpitude of the neighborhood is precisely the mass of which Christ says we are to be the leaven. Christ observed that the healthy need no physician and that he came to save sinners. It is a strange religious who abhors sinners and shuts himself or herself away from the needy. Even parish societies cannot escape bearing witness to their baptism by a corporate apostolate, whether of decent speech fostered, liturgical renewal explained, or charitable works shared in. Pope Pius XII insisted, for example, that tertiary groups, who once emphasized that their reason for existence was personal holiness and not the support of parochial and other projects, should accept some specific apostolate as the expression of personal sanctification of their fraternity.

Sometimes it is merely our presence, our face-to-face contact with the frustrated, the poor, the immoral, the retarded, the defiant, that uplifts them, for we are *living testimonials of hope.* No one is born wearing a religious garb. Hence our free assumption of the habit is a reminder of another, higher set of standards that lead to eternal justice, never-ending fulfillment, perpetual joy. But the religious, especially the superior, who forbids such apostolic contacts hides hope from the world and leaves the mass without leaven.

To be a *living rescript of the Gospel* among men is the only justification for religious life in a society that already is on the move to destroy poverty, disease, inequality.

This is the tone to be set in a religious novitiate. We cannot both be successfully launched into a life of vows and still retain the artificial props of training that held us in place before we were air-borne apostles. The purpose of these words is to establish an attitude in the reader's mind whereby the religious life may be understood not only in the useful—but partial—light of tradition, but also in the full light of the Gospel.

I have enunciated a skeletal principle. Only dialogue with each other, in and out of religious life, can put flesh on the bones. Only each community individually can understand the drive of a founder or foundress. Change for its own sake does not bespeak progress. The pages ahead may indicate some directions. I suspect many religious superiors have embarked on false tides of renewal —to their regret. Only patience and time, plus the co-operation of the total community, can evaluate the experiment. But singularly negative is the critic who decries experiment or harshly judges the occasional and inevitable failures of those who did experiment.

In Renoir's biography by his son, we read of the last days of the artist's life. He was acclaimed and his paintings prized by the best museums. Yet in an interview he had the perspective to avow, "When an artist thinks he is a genius, he is through. His only salvation is to work like a laborer without delusions of grandeur."

Thus right up to his final days a religious is not a finished product, just as the community did not completely evolve in the lifetime of a founder. The novitiate is never quite done; it is a "commencement," as the speakers use it at graduation. When a species ceases to evolve, it perishes. So a religious even in the final months of his life must work like a common laborer without delusions of grandeur. If change is hard but necessary, because of the purpose of religious life as outlined above, then the oldest members should be the most sensitive to the guiding Spirit, even if it means that they must relinquish the reins of authority they have held so long—and generally so honorably as well. In another place we shall assess their role in the community.

In these days, we might add parenthetically at this time, when democracy demands equality and scientific curiosity demands proof, religious orders must take what is spiritually profitable from these trends and sanctify and exploit them for the benefit of souls without losing grasp of the concepts of unwavering obedience and un-questioned authority. We must take away the spoils of Egypt, as the Jews in the Exodus, without longing for the leeks of self-indulgence as well. The problem stated in general terms in this opening chapter is this: each com-munity must discover in the light of its own framework and tradition how the members can be part of a perma-nently effective apostolate (because most apostolates need the support of a traditional institution) and yet have face-to-face, spontaneous contacts with needy souls (because each religious is a unique person with individ-ual capabilities and a special message to communicate to others). The purpose of the novitiate is teach tradition, create apostles, and make individual personalities flower in the context of religious life.

An analogy for nuns in particular is an observation I made once about a sister-teacher; it applies to teaching priests and brothers as well. She taught her subject well; she prepared exhaustive supplementary material. But she did not teach a love for her subject. She trained scholars, but communicated no regard or desire for scholarship. The sister could not learn from a teacher-education course in college how to be more than an institutional staff member, how to transfer an inspiration she herself had never caught. Similarly the novitiate—or rather the instructors in the novitiate—must be the vehicle of en-thusiasm. The discernment of an apt candidate is wheth-er he or she has caught the enthusiasm—not sentimen-tally, but with that kind of quiet emotion that sparks determination of the will.

I have given an example of where there might have been a failure in the novitiate—in a wider sense, all early training—in preparing a priest to lead on a spiritual plane his intellectual superiors among the laymen. I added a remark on the important balance of "institutionalism" and personal incentive in the life of a teaching nun. Now a word about the religious brothers who are coadjutors of the priests in religious orders.

Among the more foolish remarks I have heard addressed to these brothers is this, "You have come to the community to work." A man could have done as much outside a cloister if work were the touchstone of holiness. What of the aged and sick brothers who cannot work any longer? Surely their vocation is not in peril. A brother comes to religious life to save his soul, and work is only one of many means. Whereas laziness is an injustice to the community, prayer, the environment of recollection, the support of others' example and friendship all outrank work as the means to holiness. Therefore the brother who works overly-long hours, whether by choice or command, is not necessarily the most sanctified as a result.

What has this observation to do with the novitiate? I have seen too many brothers trained in novitiates as "second-class citizens." I am not referring here to the democratic trend that will probably include brothers in administration and "higher" tasks in the apostolate—this spirit is already on the move. I have reference to the present abortive training in religious life, catechism level of theological instruction (lest brothers be taken away an extra hour a day from their labors), ignorance of technical skills and the rest. Whether or not they are trained with clerical candidates is not nearly so relevant as whether they understood the *special nature* of a brother's vocation.

Nowadays with food so plentiful and cheap, many orders are closing down large-scale farm operations. With secretarial help available in many rectories and institutions, brothers are often less fit to function in that capacity. With women able to be hired as cooks and housekeepers even in rural areas and often doing a better job, brothers seem to be an anachronism. The old chestnut about "no women in the cloister" splits apart in view of the fact that diocesan clergy do not seem to suffer in virtue. (The value of brothers as domestics is more obvious in large institutions or where privacy is a more delicate matter.)

In other words, religious brothers are not so necessary in the modern, urban world for their *work*. Are we to refuse brother candidates in the future, especially if their training requires separate and costly institutions? God forbid. What I am urging is that, even if a brother never gets to be a teacher, or administrator, or liturgical commentator, or deacon in the missions, or fills any office usually reserved in his order to priests, it is, once more, not so much what he does, but what he is: a living testimonial of hope and a rescript of the Gospel. If brothers leave, I believe it is because their novitiate and early training stressed their role as workers rather than renewers of Christ-life among men. In a true sense their external works bear a closer resemblance to laymen than a priest's. Incidentally, what I have said of brothers applies equally to those communities of nuns which yet keep a distinction betwen choir-sisters and lay-sisters, who are their helpers and home-makers.

Perhaps the religious dropouts and scarcity of vocations are partially explained by the older members' unwillingness to change. If the voice of the people is the voice of God, then we must interpret the lack of vocations to the divine displeasure with those who have not been attentive to the Holy Spirit urging renewal. I am sure God will supply the Church with a new series of reformers to meet the challenge. The day may come, ten centuries from now—if the world survives—when *aggiornamento* will mean a return to hermitages, like the desert Fathers. But that would be as irrelevant now to most of the religious orders as sitting on top of a pillar, like St. Simon Stylites.

What is the purpose in drawing attention to the novitiate for religious long past the novitiate in this prefatory chapter? I wish all religious to be aware that the novitiate is the heart of the community. Its policies and products are everyone's concern. A novicemaster or -mistress is the focus of training, the midwife, of the community. The barriers and prejudices of a candidate are never so utterly lowered as in the novitiate. At no other period does a candidate give such large blocks of time to the great quest of *purpose in life.* The novitiate is the matrix of the Christ-life in the sense of the Gospel story of the person who found the pearl of great price. He sold all his goods to accumulate the money to buy this single treasure, which he left hidden in a field until he could afford it. The relevant point here is that a pearl begins in an enclosed shell where it crystallizes and grows and becomes lustrous. The shell is the novitiate, whose enclosure should be temporary and useful only for the time of formation. One cannot begin living a personally responsible life with the same endless strictures and bonds.

2 : A "Sacramental" View of the Vows

A MAN before a high court urges the Fifth Amendment so he may with impunity disregard his oath to tell the "whole truth and nothing but the truth." Two persons end their love story with a divorce or rupture of the marriage vows that should link them forever. Statesmen and soldiers and policemen promise to fulfill their duty and defend our way of life, yet use their status to amass wealth or to exert pressure or to escape prosecution or to justify violence or to exercise the "freedom" of immorality. And now religious are with greater frequency revoking their vows. All the cases cited, of course, are the exceptions in society. But the frequency of failure should be investigated and circumvented in religious life.

Before the promulgation of the present Code of Canon Law, a religious as a rule took perpetual vows after the novitiate. Now there is a "cooling-off" period of the "first vows"—or rather, a time to discover whether fervor *will* cool off. Unfortunately, whereas it did give a longer time for a religious vocation to mature, it likewise gave rise to increased defections from religious life *indirectly*. Vows become promises readily broken or dispensed from even before the term of the temporary vows is over.

As I say, indirectly a false impression is lent to the meaning of the vows by the "temporary" period. Many religious, unsure of their vocations, take vows—often at the urging of spiritual directors or even superiors—almost casually. They understand they can reach a decision later. The decision is put off and glossed over indefinitely. Rather should the novitiate be extended than admission to vows permitted. The temporariness of vows should be primarily the outlet and safety valve for the community, not the candidate. Too many superiors rate quantity above quality of vocation anyway. The mediocrity of religious today is the manifest result. Pressure is put on novicemasters and -mistresses and other superiors of the young to encourage perseverance because of the community's existing commitments to staff institutions, fill positions and make money. Top-level superiors tend to evaluate the soundness of the recruitment and training program in mere numbers and financial return. What then should the word *vow* conjure up in the idealistic imagination of the candidate?

An ancient meaning of the Latin word *sacramentum* was "oath." The classical writers, even before the Church Fathers, used *sacramentum* to describe the vow of loyalty made by soldiers at an altar to serve a particular military leader. In other words, the visible oath-taking signified their will to be their leader's man. The comparison with a sacramental sign, which gave rise to its use, is at once apparent. But there is a special parallel between the religious vows of loyalty to God and the initiatory sacrament of baptism.

It is clear in theology that the religious vows establish

one in a new and special status in the Church, yet there is no sacrament of Holy Orders involved. Beginning with baptism, every soul is constituted a member of Christ. Each additional sacrament gives the recipient a new function in the Body of Christ. As every member is not called to be a priest, not every member is called to be a religious. In either case it is a response to a specific invitation from the Head of the Body to act in a new capacity.

Adequately seen, then, even temporary vows, like each Holy Order, bespeak the recipient's lifelong will to fit into a new design of things. Of specific application here is the warning of the Lord not to swear, but answer "yes" or "no," that is, do not lightly take an oath, but be honest and sincere when you do. Do not dissemble, but let your word accurately express your intent. When an adult is baptized, or an infant with his sponsors supplying the words, he must believe and profess the faith, and he must promise to observe its commands. Even the temporarily professed must believe in the value of the specialized observance of the Gospel he is undertaking and accept all the obligations of the vows. The very numbers of religious who do not even complete their temporary commitment reinforces the suspicion that they were permitted to take first vows with many doubts and serious misgivings, but especially that they withheld their full commitment to God. The close of novitiate ends the courtship; "first vows" are not the beginning of a "trial marriage" of the candidate in his new life. Once more, superiors should either extend the time of trial or dismiss the candidate. If there is such a thing as a temporary vocation, it should probably be interpreted as referring to the time of trial. It may be true that God wishes a person to learn a religious skill or be preserved from a habit of sin or establish some religious contact for his future life as a lay person.

A secondary problem from the candidate's view is his or her desire to have *absolute* certainty of a religious vocation. Outside of express personal revelation, we have only *moral* certitude—but this is no small assurance or unsafe harbor. Moral certainty arises from the use of reason and common sense coupled with the ordinary decisions of reliable persons who have been in similar straits. Thus the customary diffidence, prudent doubts, and even occasional fears of others are guidelines for the insecure. In fact, even the doubts of vocation experienced by seasoned religious (apart from those *responsible* for the doubts due to their own lax lives and spiritual indifference!) should be relieved by the memory of their early determination to give themselves to God. The primary problem of the religious hesitant about his vocation is the inability to lift his problem occasioning doubts out of their emotional context. This point needs development in another chapter.

Another aspect of the candidate's desire for absolute certainty is his dependence upon superiors and advisers to decide for him. A nun who continually exposes doubts to a confessor and a novice who wears a path to the spiritual director's door are often reluctant to decide to give themselves to God without reserve. But no one can substitute his own will for another's. A candidate who insists on the transfer of this obligation is not a fit subject of the life of vows. But when the candidate is not even attracted to the life by a natural inclination and forces himself, after this initial attraction has disintegrated, to accept crucifixion with Christ, I believe his life of vows is very meritorious.

I have emphasized the role of superior and candidate for vows without yet describing the essential note of a religious vocation. It is the call from God as manifested through his human agents, ecclesiastical superiors. Can they err? Of course they can, but they have also the grace of office. If they thwart the operations of grace because they are lax or opportunists, then God will judge them. At least the candidate need not fear that, if he acts prudently and unemotionally to make his *own* choice, there is a danger of the loss of his soul. It is inconceivable of God and inconsistent with an adequate notion with his merciful justice that a misguided candidate suffer *ultimate* spiritual loss. True, there may be a rocky road of emotional upsets and temporary spiritual loss, but not final ruin.

To emphasize the legal aspect of vows is to define a vocation: acceptance by lawful superiors. Therefore, if a *confessor* (who can judge whether sin precludes a life of vows) and a *spiritual director* who can judge the sincerity of purpose and degree of prayer life and attitudes toward the community ideal) and the local *superior* (who can judge external behavior and reasonable tractability) concur, then a candidate has no adequate reason to delay or refuse profession. Such a man or woman simply uses unreasonable doubts to refuse to serve God.

Obviously these are general principles. Adequate counseling and individual understanding of these guidelines are not easy to procure. The three offices of confessor, director and local superior may somewhat overlap. Further, the acceptance of vows must necessarily include knowledge of the exact details of observance. Finally, even if a candidate is absolutely acceptable to lawful authority and likewise geared personally to desire to serve God, he may simply be without the courage to live in a second-rate order, as so many seem to be. However, transfer to a stricter community is not faithlessness to God, but honesty, if such a transfer is objectively made.

Religious founders themselves seem to have been beset by more doubts than most religious. How does this tally with the principles above? The founders generally were establishing new trends and new precedents. They did not have the confirmed environment of an existing community. For example, I remember a member of a cloistered order of nuns who engaged in no external apostolate. She left with permission some years ago and successfully established a modern order with foreign missions and higher schools, yet the nuns observe the same rigorous conventual life with mortification as to food and sleeping on plain boards and so on, that they observed in the totally cloistered group.

"Being fit" dawns on one slowly. It is saying repeatedly, "Yes, Lord." The evolution of a vocation might be described as *extricating* oneself from the emotional overlay and novelty of beginning to serve God and *isolating* our motives by self-examination and the scrutiny of superiors. The Constitutions of my own order stress that developed holiness is not a requirement and condition of entry to the community, by calling the order a "school of perfection." Holiness and maturity are the goal and purpose of religious life. Once more—since it cannot be said too often—the essential note is *acceptance* by ecclesiastical authority. Even the Apostles needed a three-year novitiate after Christ called them. He said clearly, "Many things I have yet to say to you, but you could not accept them now." Judas failed his novicemaster.

St. Francis of Assisi was twenty-eight years old in 1209 when he heard the words of St. Matthew's Gospel with thrilling urgency, "Go and preach that the kingdom of God is at hand." Leading up to that moment were *years of confusion and hesitation.* He learned the brevity of life when he lay sick in the prison of Perugia. He learned it is better to serve the highest Lord instead of a secondary master, when he was on the way to war with Walter of Brienne. He learned that a life of personal gratification is vacuous when he was surfeited with the "gay science" of carousing. He learned self-discipline when he kissed the leper and tried the life of a beggar for a time in Rome. He learned detachment and courage when he accepted public disownment by his father and humiliation by the townsfolk. There were months of moody retreat in caves and finally two years of trial at San Damiano, rebuilding churches and chapels. But once St. Francis made his own decision—there was little if any direct counseling from others, if the histories are right—he did not make a temporary vow.

Many religious who have decided for insufficient reasons to forsake the religious state simply consider their past experience in the community as a closed issue. It is true that some are better off and more likely to save their souls outside the community—whether the defection is due to laxity, or a defect of training, or the forceful persuasion of others that vows be pronounced, despite the candidate's disabilities. But in any of these instances it is clear that such a person must *answer for his actions* on the day of judgment. Leaving the order ends certain external activities but not the development of one's spiritual life. On the day of particular judgment we shall receive the light to know whether we had sufficient reason to reject the favor of a vocation, and whether we lacked love and courage through our own fault.

It is often said that God's call is "only" an invitation and we are not bound to answer positively, just as the young man in the Gospel who refused the Lord's call and went away, because he was attached to his riches. Apart from the Gospel describing him as going away "sad," the narrative does not reveal Christ's reaction so clearly. But his divine disappointment would be obvious enough from the full understanding of a vocation as the flowering of our baptism.

God wishes to constitute a baptized person in a new status with a new spiritual function: to live a Christ-life as witness to the belief and hope in resurrection and glory in a manner more intense than the average Christian, because the context of the community makes that witnessing easier to achieve. Refusal thwarts the operation of a grace destined for us eternally. In heaven or hell the candidates will grasp how much less intense was the image of Christ in the soul than God planned it to be.

The several references to baptism and its flowering in the religious state, to the analogy between a vocation and sacraments, and to the image of Christ in the soul of a religious need an alignment at this point. In many senses a vocation is a real mystery of grace. Baptism initiates the soul to the life of God; the baptized is a member of Christ's Body as he shares in that life. The life of God, of course, is the "internal operations" of the Trinity. Let us describe briefly that operation which both links and separates the Persons.

Eternally—hence now also—God the Father generates the Son. He expresses himself with the Word, the Second

Person. The gaze of the Two is "personalized" as the Spirit. The Holy Spirit is the "crystallized," mutual love between the Father and Son. The philosophical problems attendant upon such a simplified statement of the mystery are surely complex. The point to be made is that the Persons' life was not consummated in some dim past—as many seem to conceive the mystery.

When the soul shares in God's life through baptism, he is swept up into the bosom of the Three and participates according to the measure of his capacity. The specific action of the Trinity indwelling the soul is the re-production of the Son by the Father through the Holy Spirit. We are a kind of *repetition of the Incarnation* of Christ as an "external operation" of the Trinity. This is such an awesome truth that a human mind could not conceive the dignity of his place in the universe without the revelation of Sacred Scripture and the pronouncement of the Church.

The prototype, of course, of our human share in the divine life of the Trinity is the Incarnation of the Son in the womb of the Virgin Mary through the action of the Holy Spirit. God, the Most High, overshadowed her and what was born of her was God's Son and the most perfect human vessel of grace or God's Trinitarian life. Our personal intensity of sanctifying grace may be described as the clarity of Christ's image in us. And this image of Christ is two-fold: 1) our "Trinitarian" life, whereby we internally strive to be perfect "as our heavenly Father is perfect," and 2) our external "Christ-life," whereby we strive to reproduce the earthly activities and motivation of Jesus.

This is not an easy doctrine, but it is at the heart of Christianity. All other doctrines are in consequence of it and receive their theological energy from it. One theology professor said the explanation of the Trinity and our share in its life is so sacred, that one ought both to write and read about it kneeling!

Religious, then, are called to exhibit Christ-life in external ways through the apostolates of their community. Even totally cloistered orders are true Christs-incarnate again when they exhibit that aspect of Christ's life which was "hidden with God" and those periods when he prayed alone in the garden or in the desert apart from men. Such religious are likewise fulfilling an apostolate, that is, they are "sent" to the world to bear witness to Christ-among-us. They are part of the body of Christ alive in the world, the sign of its hope and the leaven of the mass in a particular way. Their vocation, as that of all religious, is the flowering of the baptism. They are externally reproducing Christ's life and interpreting it for our times.

Whether by historical accident or ancient insight into this fact, religious orders commonly observe many parallels with baptismal ritual in their profession ceremonies. The candidate is born spiritually in some sense. In the order as in the ancient Church, a *scrutinium* or evaluation by the community, of the candidate's worthiness, is conducted. The spiritual family gathers around because the new life being added will affect them—hence baptisms were originally conferred in the Church during the crowded Holy Saturday ceremonies. Witnesses of the profession required by Church law are analogous to the sponsors at baptism. Only at the end of the catechumenate was the baptizand taught the "Our Father," because God was not his father in the full sense of grace before; similarly only now can the professed make demands for support upon the superior. The Creed is repeated by the baptizand with the bystanders renewing their faith; the candidate vows his belief in a special form of the evangelical life as able to sanctify his soul for glory. In both ceremonies the ritual is initiatory to further offices in the community. The incidentals of a special garment, candles, and the like reinforces the parallel. Perhaps the most striking parallel from the viewpoint of the new Christ-life in either case is the remission of all temporal punishment due to sins for which the candidate has genuine remorse. So striking is the acceptance of God's call by religious profession, say the theologians, that it merits the restoration of baptismal innocence!

3 : Perseverance Depends Upon Love of the World

PRAYER is hard work and the true spirit of prayer a rare achievement even in religious life, although a religious tyro finds it easy at first. A parade example of first fervor threatened by the grind of daily prayer is Eirik, son of Olav, in Sigrid Undset's *Son Avenger*. Eirik entered a Minorite novitiate after a wayward life. He was so taken by his new life and the emotional response elicited by its novelty that he asked and received permission to remain in the conventual church after night-time matins until the morning hour of prime.

Particularly in summer his entry into the cool, dark church refreshed him as much as a plunge into the fiord did in his former way of life. He found a kind of sensual delight in watching the figures in the stained-glass windows slowly come to life with the first light. He looked forward to the greater holidays when the entire Divine Office would be sung according to the local custom. During meditation his imaginative mind conceived the mysteries of Christianity as an attic of locked treasure chests, to which religious life alone could supply the key. At those lonely hours of vigil, when the sanctuary was deserted by everyone else, Eirik scourged himself, taking physical satisfaction in the heroic punishment his strong, young body could endure in reparation for his past sins.

His maimed finger precluded Eirik from applying as a candidate for the priesthood, but his fervor had grown so white-hot that he accepted the setback with good grace and decided to stay on as a brother candidate. He was temporarily comforted when the novice master observed that St. Francis never received ordination, but remained a deacon all his life. Then the chill, shortening days of autumn came to the north country.

Eirik missed the warm furs and blankets at night as he lay under the thin coverlet. The church grew rather cold now and the nights of watching endless. His brain seemed to freeze into apathy during meditation. He no longer found consolation and sweetness during the dismal vigils. The Latin psalms were, after all, in a wholly meaningless language. Eirik did not even approach the tabernacle as closely anymore, for fear of the Almighty One enthroned there who seemed to have withdrawn his support.

The cold of the dormitory prevented the young man from finding his proper rest; he always seemed weary, his brain dull. He remembered how in his layman's life he would return home from hard labor and the cold to warm his hands at the crackling fire with cheerful company. Now he foresaw years of the lonely cold and the grand silence. His spiritual directors told him to pray; he fasted and prayed in silent agony. But he rejected the interior voice that could have inspired him to sustain this first trial in detachment. Instead he thought of his family's prosperous farm, the hunting and fishing and happy gatherings. None of these was evil; the world was good. Eirik left, of course.

So many lessons for the neophyte and his directors arise from this true-to-life tale penned by Sigrid Undset. Eirik could not distinguish between faith and consolations as the true support of prayer life. With his newly discovered spiritual outlook on life, neither Satan nor his own nature tempted him to return to the wicked and dissolute life he had led. He rather saw the world as it truly is, beautiful and inviting and wholesome. But Eirik did not see through this allure to the greater attraction possible in religious life.

The whole point of a vocation is not the rejection of "the world" because it is evil, but precisely because it is so good and beautiful that it interferes with the soul's ascent to God. (The meaning of "worldliness" in contemporary religious jargon deserves a special chapter of treatment later). Once we have seen through the world and beyond it to its Maker, we begin to love the world and desire to transform it into a new Paradise and baptize its pagan element out of existence. The wholesome religious, even in the secluded monasteries, does not despise the world but stands in the midst of its activity proclaiming the value of a higher dedication. Another name for this mature attitude is zeal for souls.

The longer a person perseveres in grace, the more he is concerned with the conversion of others. The indifference of a shepherd of souls to non-Catholics in the parish boundaries, the abhorrence by the religion teacher of the recalcitrant student, the routine handling of cases by the social service worker bespeak a lack of zeal for the spiritually helpless. Since no one grows in one virtue without increasing in the others, perseverance in the religious state grows in pace with our love of souls. "Give me souls; take away the rest!" was the explicit motto of many saints.

Because good as well as evil diffuses itself, the good religious will desire as a matter of course to share with others his good fortune, which is intimate contact with God. The manifest proof of this is the eagerness with which young religious recruit others and seek to influence them to accept a religious calling. Conversely, how many older religious lose this initiative and even make it a "matter of conscience" not to steer young and hopeful vocations into their own community, lest those religious be burdened with another problem besides their own laxity!

If Eirik had been counseled properly, he might have stayed on in the community. In the story his superior apparently thought a directive to further prayer enough. A parallel is the counsel given by directors to religious tempted against purity to pray more at the times of temptation. Thus the besieged person's attention turns more fully on the dangerous area. The saints assure us —from the vantage point of their mature experience— that meditation on the suffering of the Crucified is the greatest deterrent against a sin of impurity. But for the sincere beginner a temptation rises not from the weakness of the soul, but from the strength of the body.

Eirik's problem was mostly natural: confinement, boredom, physical exhaustion, loneliness and the rest. A beginner away for the first time from home, when he enters military service or college, often shares the same experience. It is true that an experienced vocation could find support in intensified prayer and make the natural problems mentioned the occasion of greater spiritual experience. The superior failed to point out the "first-fervor" pitfall to Eirik, and was probably unwise in permitting an unseasoned religious to adopt an intense spiritual activity that left no room for further development. He was also doomed to failure because there was no interior foundation for the externals of his prayer life. Eirik was permitted to run before he could walk. Nor did the superior point out that Eirik would not be *rejecting* a good world and his family, but *serving* them by the support of his prayers and the witness of his reformed life until that day of glory when they would be reunited in heaven. Natural means also must be used to combat natural problems, which become supernatural only because they arise in the context of religion.

Beginners (and often the older religious) will never arrive at emotional maturity until they accept themselves unglossed, as inescapable children of nature, with weaknesses that may never be eradicated in their lives. They must understand that God does not expect success as the world of politics, business or education demands a successful product. The religious is more akin to the professional research scientist, who is not forced to create a marketable product. His labor and technical training and dedication justify his salary. So for the religious true spiritual success consists primarily in the desire and dedication to perfection, even if he does not achieve it because of some hidden reason—perhaps even a mystery of grace itself. To live with zeal despite the frustrations of our personal experience is assuredly acceptable to God. I do not refer to sins which preclude the religious profession, but to the inability to learn spiritual techniques of prayer or be rid of indeliberate sins. The testy and cranky religious, who must confess his daily irritations over and over again, yet struggles against them and makes them the occasion of trusting more in Christ's purifying power than his own effort, is closer to God than a person whose natural endowments and early training do not give rise to impatience.

If one leg of perseverance is accepting ourselves for what we are realistically, then the other is admitting simultaneously both that we can improve ourselves and that we are worth improving. The existentialist, Victor Frankl, described life in a Nazi concentration camp, where perseverance meant physical survival, just as a religious' perseverance means spiritual survival. Frankl observed that those who survived were not necessarily the physically strong, but rather those who had a purpose in their existence and hence a reason for survival. Thus the tempted and desolated religious might conclude that he could save his soul as well, perhaps more easily, as a lay person. But survival as a religious should always be tempered by the knowledge of our special purpose of existence. Once more enters the concept of religious vows as the extension of our baptismal vows.

The story is told of a nun who entered the postulancy at an early age. By the time of profession saccharine emotions (as evidenced by the vacuous stare of her tearfilled eyes), coupled with an undoubtedly honest response to God drove her through the early days of training. Her appointment to the missions moved her with apostolic efforts equal to experienced missioners. Then her prolonged contacts and awareness of the love shared by the married natives and their families, plus their relative undress because of the tropical climate, contrived to drive a wedge into her protective armor. She apparently felt cheated of normal human love, which she could not have known because of her early entry into religious life.

However, it was the fault of the community almost entirely that she was never taught to replace the normal, face-to-face, warm, human contacts of her natural family with similar ones in the convent. She probably would never have succumbed to envying the natives if she had had her own legitimate human contacts. This, once more, has reference to the earlier chapter that touches on the necessary balance between the institution and the individual.

Someone may counter that she was not ready for the convent at the age she entered—a plea of many parents. Whereas this is true in individual cases, the rule-of-thumb is to come when you hear the call. Did Christ not warn that the dead should bury the dead? The time to answer "yes" is the moment when the grace is offered. (I often wonder whether some of the many Catholic marriages that fail today are traceable to the fact that one partner had been given such a grace and rejected it.) The nun in question needed affection from her sisters, counseling about her natural problem, and the conviction that her life had a purpose of existence that outweighed other considerations. Again, perseverance and zeal for souls are irrevocably linked in a dedicated religious soul. Religious communities will continue to founder and, by comparison with the Catholic population, even grow smaller, until they understand the natural needs of their members as seen by the stories of the nun, of Eirik, of Victor Frankl.

"First fervor" is the initial stumbling block of perseverance, but it is critical enough. Far more burdensome to the individual and to the community is the uncertainty of perseverance in the professed religious. For them the schedule is mere external routine. It doesn't seem to help to examine one's conscience. The repetitious muttering of the rosary is seldom energized by the reflection that other devout souls claim for themselves. The mechanical and expressionless recitation of the Office seems to ignore the very God in chapel whom the religious is trying to contact. The subject matter of meditation seems so unrelated to practical life. Spiritual directors seem in such a hurry to get a session done with. Confessors seem to tell one just to keep up the good work. Spiritual books outline principles and techniques of spiritual growth that are long stereotyped. The pious proverbs sanctioned by centuries of mouthing infuriate the frustrated soul. Was there ever a religious without this creeping disillusion? What answer may be given here and now as a practical stop-gap until the religious has time to draw on long-term sources and recoup her temporary loss of fervor?

The temporary stop-gap is to act as if you had no doubts. A decision that may affect one's whole future is never justified in being made when a religious is depressed, any more than a decision made at the time of extreme elation is valid, for neither extreme represents the ordinary state of mind. Objective decisions need many days and weeks and often months of relatively tranquil spiritual life, if the choice is to be intelligent. For this reason one does not wisely come to the retreat before vows with the intention to decide during the retreat if profession is to be made. (If the doubt is about some lesser choice, as one's qualifications for a new apostolate being offered by the superior or the prudence of embarking on new studies, then less time of tranquillity is required for a soul-searching choice. The supposition here, of course, is that the subject has some control of the future, which is not often verified in religious life, especially in the routine use of personnel.)

Meanwhile the religious must live his or her life to the hilt with maximum conviction that the externals of religious life must be more than merely endured, but fulfilled with alert cooperation. He should continue all his spiritual exercises in cold faith without the self-seeking desire to have uplift and satisfaction. After all, the spiritual exercises are not evil, they are good. Merit, which is—granted—a secondary motive, is being accumulated. He is being likened to Christ, who called out despairingly from Gethsemani and Calvary. Therefore one must *act as if he did have all the strength necessary.* Why? *The fact we are yet seeking God with concern means exactly that we have found him.* Even the imperfect can find God. Perhaps the imperfect may never on earth experience a close divine contact or master exalted spiritual techniques. Five years or fifty may find one sluggish. But some religious will save their souls and live a true Christ-life, even without notable apostolic success, only because they never stopped trying.

Consider the work of St. Paul. His letters manifest his frustration over carousing Corinthians and imputations that he was profiteering from his preaching. Further, practically all the towns where he preached in Asia Minor lost the faith in subsequent centuries, except for handfuls of Christians today. The brilliant faith of North Africa under St. Cyprian and St. Augustine, so productive of saintliness and scholarship, fell before the enforced indoctrination of Islam in the seventh century. North Africa remains Moslem today. The fact that our own nation may someday fall prey to false idealism which could destroy the future of the Church should not inhibit our order's apostolate; this is obvious. The same is true of our personal frustration that while we are preaching salvation to others by our religious life, we ourselves seem to be gasping for a full breath of spiritual oxygen. Remember how the Jesuits gave testimony to the Mohawks and Hurons for years with only a relatively small number of conversions. Particularly in Huronia they saw their labors disintegrate. Wholesale conversions finally began to occur, but disease, unscrupulous white traders, and slaughter by other hostile tribes decimated the faithful. Of the approximately forty thousand Huron Indians only about three hundred survived after twenty-four years of evangelization! The sustaining thought of the Jesuits' perseverance was surely the conviction of the value of what they did, even though they saw their apostolate disintegrate about them.

The lesson for the individual religious doubtful of his vocation is twofold. First, in the perspective of larger movements in the Church, of which our vocation is only a small part, and seen against the background of frustrations of apostles and martyrs, our personal problems do not loom so large. We are always in danger of such introspection that we magnify our needs and failures out of proportion. We develop an exaggerated need of self-approval and tranquillity, forgetting that only the violent take the kingdom of heaven by storm. Certainly the graces given Paul, Cyprian and the Jesuit martyrs are not denied to us—that is, if not the chance to die heroically, at least to live so.

Second, if the individual's doubt arises from the fact the community seems to lag behind others in the overhauling of the Church or is, at best, a generally run-down mechanism, one fact stands out. Even in a third-rate order with few knowledgable leaders, an individual is not prevented from achieving spiritual success and perfecting himself, apostolically speaking, even if few such contacts are open. Although the community's corporate Christ-life is confused and weak, the member's Christ-life may be intense. Indeed, that may be why God placed that member there: to be a living testimonial of hope to one's fellow religious. Is there greater charity than this? A more fundamental question is, obviously, whether such a person is making an accurate assessment of the situation or is merely the echo of a group of disgruntled religious, who reinforce each other in their unhappiness. In any event, God apparently wanted us where we have gravitated, even if his providence was as lowly a fact as being raised in a parish served by our particular order. It seems a little presumptuous to thwart this providence, except for external causes as ill-health or the proven desire to enter a stricter life.

The story is told of a novice who had once been in a war-detention camp in Europe. He came to America and entered a religious community of moderate asceticism. While others, younger than he, were having a hilarious time during recreation, for example, he eschewed their company for solitary walks in the garden with a prayer book in his hands. He often commented that he had slept on bare boards in winter in the detention-camp, but had a comfortable mattress and blanket in the novitiate. He was finally told it was perfectly legitimate to sleep on the floor with the windows wide open, if he thought it was essential to his spiritual progress. He transferred to a stricter religious order, but left that one, too.

I remember a gardener who was devoted to his greenhouse. Along one wall of glass he had strung up a *triangularis* plant, whose botanical identity has long evaded my memory. He watered the soil and cultivated the unsightly thing from time to time with singular patience. When the plant finally bloomed one summer, the bud began to "tremble" about eight o'clock in the evening until it opened completely and filled the greenhouse with unbelievable fragrance. By midnight its glory was consumed, as if the very passion of blooming destroyed it. It drooped over into lifelessness in just four hours. The *triangularis* is not unlike a "victim soul" persevering for years because he loves his order and wishes to uplift it. I forgot to mention that the gardener tended his plant for twenty-nine years before it bloomed the first time.

4 : Up-dating, or Belonging to the Present

THE RELIGIOUS belongs to God in a special way. Because love is a two-way street, God belongs to the religious in a special way, too. St. Paul remarked in his first letter to the Corinthians, "All things are yours because you are Christ's and Christ is God's." In our technological and rapidly changing world, we have less of a problem of being "contaminated" by the world than merely keeping up with its good advances. Everything wholesome in creation can be a resource for the modern religious, yet I have heard of a superior of students on the college level who protested that his subjects should study Shakespeare "like a doctor studies diseases," from a controlled distance in order not be infected!

The day when priests and religious were the only professional educators, lawyers, social workers and even scientists, is long gone. These professions were the Church's contributions to humanity in the past; they continue to occur, however, in the great mission territories of the world remaining. But they were always only secondary. The rise of Protestant educational institutions and Protestant caritative works, some centuries ago, followed by the sociological efforts of secular governments, gave Catholic professionals less cause to think these areas belonged to them exclusively. That we are less needed in these fields today can provide the freedom religious need to be effective in the primary task of evangelization. We ought not, however, immediately conclude that the logical end of traditional apostolates has come.

We are neither to sidestep the passing world nor get swept away by its rush. God wants us to keep our proper and right position among men. I would like to be able to say we belong in front of the world as its leaders everywhere. However pious this would sound, religious and priests lack the skills in a departmentalized world to lead it in very many fields. By our presence, however, we can turn the direction of the passing world, lift it by our moral persuasion, and especially baptize it by our prudent use even in the areas of technology and entertainment. Thus one order of men produces an educational film about how to assess the artistic merits and moral quantities of films produced for entertainment. A group of women religious print their own books in order more cheaply to disseminate Catholic literature in a door-to-door apostolate. Such apostolates get into the marrow of laymen's lives. The day may come when such activities will lose their efficacy and outlive their own need. Then the religious should forsake them. Religious men are to be the "specialists" in the Church, just as the diocesan clergy are to be the "regular troops."

It is seriously to be doubted, for example, that the parishes acquired by some orders when certain areas were religiously underdeveloped or designated as mission territories should continue to be operated by male religious unless certain conditions are verified: The parish may be the ordinary apostolate for which the community was founded, the church may be historically connected with the community in a special way, the church may be the dissemination point for special information or studies, the church may require a large body of confessors for the care of pilgrims and transients, or be the gathering place of lay-groups under the spiritual tutelage of the order, and so on. Certainly the criterion of religious remaining in parishes because they are a steady source of income is insufficient. God supplies the needs of those who do his will. Does the providence of God stop operating for the religious order after the founder and first few heroic souls die?

I have heard of a group of sisters who operate an exclusive retirement home for the aged. Only about twenty may be cared for at a time; each client has a charming suite and patio with a beautiful view overlooking the city. Several sisters and even more lay persons care for the "patients." Needless to say, only the wealthy can afford it. The lucrative system supports the other more plebeian apostolates of the community. A large Catholic university was similarly under fire, when their lay teachers' salaries were significantly lower than their associates in non-Catholic schools. Yet the university had a staggering surplus after the annual budget was balanced; the surplus was used for the worthy purpose of supporting the order's foreign missions. The point is that "justice and peace have kissed each other," to borrow from the psalms. Is it right to impose our poverty upon lay persons on Friday, when salary checks are due, and preach social justice on Sunday, when the homily is due? Perhaps the members of the community were unaware of this problem at first, hence they alone can judge themselves. Nor should donations by sincere benefactors (or from those who seek the tax deductions) be the occasion of lay interference in the community's operations, for example, in the endowments of colleges and the largesse of alumni associations.

The prototype of American nuns, Mother Seton, is a case in point. She was a brilliant hostess to General Washington and other famous Americans, wealthy, talented, and happily married—not the usual antecedents of the nunnery. Her contact with a Catholic family in Italy, where she was nursing her now-penniless husband till he died, resolved her to convert. Back in the United States, her family refused her any financial aid because of her new faith. She opened a boarding house, took in sewing from her former friends and was able to help the poor out of her own indigence. Subsequently she opened the first parish school in the United States at Baltimore. From the beginning sprang a religious community caring for hospitals, orphanages, leprosaria, parish schools. Apparently Mother Seton, whose personal poverty and suffering is legend now, did not count on financial security. It seems as if God *is* actually able to care for his spouses and to produce benefactors out of his sleeve as they are needed! If Mother Seton were alive today, I do not imagine she would drag her feet in the up-dating race to save souls.

The point of *aggiornamento* for communities is not simply to change, but to discern why they were founded. If a community was founded, for example, to spread devotion to a mystery of Our Lord, then it alone can evaluate its own apostolates in the light of that foundation. True, the Church speaks for God and, indirectly, for the founder. Therefore the Church can re-direct the energy of the community. But if the community propels itself, only its members are to blame if it becomes faceless and identical with other communities, or with the diocesan clergy, in the case of male religious. Too many of us do not really know who we are or what we are. We do not know where we have been historically or where we are going apostolically. Up-dating for religious, especially the older communities, means more of going back to recapture the past and to reset it into the future with greater relevance. The leaders of the community primarily must engender this view of up-dating, for only they are experienced and in authority simultaneously. I have heard of one discerning provincial who first had a "chapter," so to speak, of younger delegates of subjects from all over his province. Then he led the dialogue between the older and younger groups to fuse their viewpoints.

One nun of only recent vintage suggested to me the very charitable observation that young religious ought not be hostile to the older ones, implying when the latter die, at last progress will be born. These older members are to be loved and respected for their pioneer role and heroic service, often without sufficient training and our present stress on education. It is poor taste and irreligious for the younger element to decry the "simple obedience" that took these pioneers into uncharted seas without a compass. They cling to the old because they love the community and its traditions, not because they dislike the new breed. The "angry young men and women" must also begin with the presumption that the "old guard" is sincere and not merely contrary! Since charity is the chief mark of a Christian, up-dating will be a farce and hypocrisy—even where objectively the change is needed

—unless charity perdures. The tide of time will wash away the old and the change will come perforce, but it is a strange victory if mutual support and charitable understanding are washed away, too.

Part of the problem of *aggiornamento* is to define balance without compromise, efficiency without laxity. In the day of air-conditioners and electric shavers and television, sometimes there is only a hair's weight of difference between the truly useful and merely convenient. And if the psychological studies are valid, then sometimes a luxury, like air-conditioning, makes an individual religious more productive of spiritual good when grace builds on nature. Another example is the value of a television for a chaplain living alone; its proper use may save him from excessive visiting of lay persons in their homes because of his humanly lonely life. Thus the problem of up-dating has also a personal impact. Each person must assess in the light of his own spiritual life and natural needs whether a typewriter, wristwatch, air-conditioner and all the rest is necessary and fruitful. The old maxims of mortification may never be set aside. It is likewise dangerous to re-interpret mortification merely on the mental level, as if corporal discipline were antiquated, or if the pace of contemporary life were mortification enough.

Conjure up a picture of a dozen women religious in a convent chapel, or men religious at a metropolitan house of studies. The noisy traffic, and children playing, and all the commerce of human life filtering through the open windows contrive to make meditation impossible. If the chapel is small and the air close, certainly it would be better to air-condition. One might plead that this is laxity. In some instances it might be. The religious must decide whether it is more important to pray well and *con-*

tact God or sit on their perspiring haunches and contact no one.

All this points up an urgent problem of up-dating, namely, that more must be left to individual convictions. It is true the initial profession of vows commits one to accept the general Constitutions and Rule and precepts of superiors. But we are such children of Adam that imposition of a community regimen reduces our personal commitment to religion, our sense of responsibility to take on mortification, and our drive to discipline ourselves—which is the only kind of mortification that God accepts. Even "common mortifications," as it were, and imposed disciplines are useless to the individual soul if they are not made personal convictions.

Therefore modernization, the uses of technology, changing concepts of poverty must be made more personal, because only an individual can determine that hair's weight of difference. Assuredly everything must be done with permission, but the letter of the law can kill the expressing of legitimate needs. In practice greater emphasis must be placed on the local superior's interpreting the general law of the community, and on the provincial's doing this for his territory. What applies to one nation does not necessarily apply to another. The use of an automobile, taken for granted in one area so that the religious do not bother lay persons to transport them everywhere, may be truly a violation of poverty in a foreign country. Just as the Church is in a trend toward decentralization, so that the bishops can use their grace of office to operate prudently, the religious orders need the same de-centralization. Naturally, abuses will creep in; that is why there must be visitors. It is precisely when the burden of sanctification is placed on the provincial and local superior more squarely, and upon the individual member more directly, that the healthy sense of achievement and responsibility will be perceived more deeply. Whereas each person, in the area of his office or competence, must look into his own soul more carefully, absolute obedience and unquestioning loyalty to command, after the subject's views are respectfully presented, must prevail—otherwise the vow is a farce. A closer external bond between poverty and obedience will be reinforced in the contemporary world of the active religious than ever before in the history of religious orders. Meanwhile the hue and cry of traditionalists, which is bound to be raised, will serve the community as a balance. To be sure, were there not lax religious in every community in the past? A little credit must be given to the sincerity of young religious entering the community nowadays. No one enters religion to become lax, but to save his soul, serve God and live the Christ-life. The training of the young must be different, but to achieve ancient objectives.

It is related of Father Maximilian M. Kolbe, O.F.M. Conv., a Polish Franciscan, that his youthful preoccupation with things mechanical and scientific was coupled with the desire to glorify the Mother of God in the order. The excesses of the Italian Masons, observed while he was studying in Rome, led Maximilian to form, in 1917, the Militia of the Immaculate—a society now spread all over the world with a membership of more than 2,000,000. To keep the originally small group cohesive he began to publish a bulletin in the sanatorium to which he had been sent, apparently to die—for he had returned from Rome in the advanced stages of tuberculosis and was hemorrhaging seriously. Somehow or other

Father Maximilian never got around to dying; in fact, he began the great work of his life with just one lung remaining.

Talk about up-dating and using current technology and science for the salvation of souls! The little press at Grodno, Poland, worked by a single brother, grew in about twelve years to the most expert publishing house in all of Central Europe. With a donation of land he built the barracks-like dormitories and chapel and printshops and dining rooms. The primitive buildings were appropriate to the poor country trying to achieve national status after the First World War. When the Nazis invaded Poland in 1939, they found also a bindery, a hundred-bed hospital, a school for candidates, training shops, a novitiate, an electric plant, a firehouse, a radio station and an airport from which to deliver their daily newspaper of 150,000 circulation to every part of the country. Father Maximilian was planning to make movies of a religious nature with the best stars of Europe and to operate a television station as soon as it became practical. His community numbered about seven hundred after twelve years. They printed in ten different languages, including Arabic—sports journals, the *Little Knight* for children, pamphlets, books, and especially the monthly *Knight of the Immaculate,* a magazine with over a million circulation in a nation of thirty million people! Meanwhile Father Maximilian had spent a few years in Japan repeating his project for the Japanese. He founded the Japanese province and a printing press while teaching temporarily in the diocesan seminary at Nagasaki. Father Maximilian returned to Poland for the triennial chapter to be caught up in the war and executed at Auschwitz with other "enemies of humanity."

Despite this wealth of equipment and the technological know-how that enabled the brothers to hold hundreds of patents, their personal poverty was uncompromising —yet nothing was too elaborate or expensive for God and Our Lady and the needs of souls. He spoke of "Brother Ink" and "Sister Press" as St. Francis spoke of the flowers and animals. When challenged sharply by a critic who said St. Francis would be horrified by the Friars' possession of such equipment, Father Maximilian demurred and said the saint would roll up his sleeves and pitch in. Lest the priests and brothers become merely robots on an assembly line amid the clatter of machines, they were periodically transferred so they might find one area best suited to their talents and geared to their own attraction. Likewise they were trained to understand the whole operation, rather than just some small process.

The rest of the incredible story of Father Maximilian is equally pointed, but not germane to the discussion at hand. We learn from this apostolic life that assembly lines, sports journals, television, airplanes and electric dishwashers can both relate to our own sanctity and be used for the sanctification of others. It is analogous to sisters and priests teaching on secular campuses (even the term "secular" is somewhat reprehensible in the context in which many Catholic educationists use it). An American proverb goes, "If you can't beat them, then join them." That is to say, use the present world to bear witness to the future world. Be a symbol of hope and ultimate justice for all. Baptize public education, entertainment, politics, and sociology. Do not make it sickly pietistic, for this is not true religion, but make these areas in which piety is operative, for it is a gift of the Holy Spirit.

Thus seminarians and postulants should not be forbidden television, but taught—why not in a regular course? —to analyze the shallow, the provocative, the cloying, the suggestive, the merely entertaining. Such a course is likely to teach them more than the typical speech or homiletics course I have observed. Sisters' and seminarians' theology ought not to stress only how we differ from Protestants or Jews, but also how we agree. The lives of religious founders or innovators or dissidents ought not to be a list of spiritual crimes and heresies, but also a sympathetic understanding of their confusion and spiritual torment. These are examples from the fields of film, television and theology, whereby we admit in a *practical* way that those without our religious convictions can be sincerely dedicated to their professions and save their souls—even while our realization of the *greater difficulty* of achieving union with God without our sacramental system should make us all the more zealous for their souls.

Certainly no small part of *aggiornamento* for the perceptive religious and priest is viewing, with many a "mea culpa," the more profound faith and back-breaking dedication of lay persons, including non-Catholics, to the causes of religion. A non-Catholic astronaut who prays aloud in space; a non-Catholic high-school student who leads public prayer outside the class to protest the anti-religious decisions of the Supreme Court; a non-Catholic woman who spends her widowhood chaperoning dances, picking up isolated choir members, driving incapacitated parishioners to church, teaching Sunday school, working at bazaars, visiting the sick—these persons are taking the kingdom of heaven by storm and winning the heart of God. It will take a great deal of up-dating, united with a great deal of the Christ-life, to equal such persons, then draw them lovingly into the true fold of the Good Shepherd.

I remember how affected was a religious priest preaching a mission in a rural parish. He saw the muddy front yards of the farm folks he visited, the bare, scrubbed floors of the houses which boasted little furniture and only a kitchen coal stove to heat the whole house. That priest came away spiritually refreshed, grateful for his comparative "affluence," and rededicated to his vow of poverty. If young religious postulants and novices could be exposed to tenement houses, rural poverty, one-room schools, lines of sweaty men and women punching clocks at the end of an August workday, they might be more inclined to bless the God of goodness, who called them from the middle-class comfort from which we have mostly arisen. Let them look at the sandwiches in the lunch pails of workmen when they sit down to a hot lunch. Let them smell the institutional odors of orphanages and prisons when they recreate in their garden— especially if the house of training be a converted mansion in the country (that curse of twentieth-century religious). It is hard to say whether the community or the individual needs more up-dating, which is another word for contact with reality and living in the present.

5 : "By This Shall All Men Know . . ."

Surely the worst sin of religious, taken as a group, is the lack of kindness to their own. It expresses itself in jealousy over others promotions, petty snubs for real or supposed offenses against oneself, clever asides about the failings of others, coolness that extends over days and months, studied disinterest in the apostolic efforts of others, depreciation of their successes. This list is not exhaustive. The names of fraternal uncharitableness are legion.

I suppose that because few of us are ever guilty of startling crimes as murder, fornication, and arson—plus the fact that laity and we ourselves would like to think of the community as a big, happy family—failures in love stand out the more. Yet Our Lord made this virtue the mark of identity of his own: "By this will all men recognize you are my followers, namely, that you love each other." This phrase is at once an encomium and an indictment. Alcoholics we pity, the proud we discount, the unchaste we commiserate. (Their weaknesses are so manifest that we feel almost superior and self-righteous; perhaps we look so favorable by the comparison.) But the judgment of the Lord is upon those who strike a discordant note in the community. "The Lord hates six things, but he loathes the seventh . . . the person who sows discord among brothers."

Because our society is outstanding in its ability to broadcast sex into every area of life, preachers decry *impurity* and spiritual directors label it the worst of sins and make it co-terminous with "immorality"—originally an unrestricted ethical concept. Religious teachers are so well indoctrinated themselves about custody of the eyes and the "angelic" virtue and the superiority of soul over body in the human composite, that their students acquire a somewhat distorted picture of their relationship with God. The commandments are listed in Sacred Scripture in the order of their objective importance—our duties toward God, then to parents as representing God, then our reverence for human life, then the prohibition of adultery, and so on. Hence there are objectively worse sins than impurity (of course, each commandment admits the possibility of grave and slight matter). On the positive side, Christ repeats the supreme commandment of the Old Testament; to love God entirely, and our neighbor as ourselves. The point of these words is not to minimize the guilt of impurity, but to show that *deliberate* sins of uncharitableness outweigh even mortal sins of impurity—not in gravity of matter, but generally in *malice*. The maliciously uncharitable person may be very indifferent to spiritual growth and perfunctory in his duties without commiting mortal sin, whereas every confessor can attest to the misery of the sincere and dedicated person who is yet trying to make the giant step to self-mastery, yet whose sins stem from weakness and not malice. Maybe Christ had this in mind when he remarked that publicans and harlots were entering the kingdom of God before the Pharisees. Is this because the obvious sins tend to make one more humble and easier to live with?

I have read that the fifth superior of the Society of Jesus, Claudius Aquaviva, polled the separate opinions of his best moralists and inquired what *objectively* mortal sins were committed by religious. The entire group, it is related, labeled uncharitableness against one's fellows as the most common of the possibly grave offenses against God. At first examination this sounds somewhat belabored and excessive—as if someone were trying to underscore a specific point out of just proportion. Yet it is true, once again, that the *mortal* sins possible against the vows of poverty, chastity and obedience are very rare, whether from conviction or the lack of opportunity, I cannot say. Many mortal sins, however, are possible against charity in every community. If they are not so judged in one's confession, it is because these sins are cloaked in various ways; hence the poll of the Jesuit General concerned objectively mortal sins, not subjective assessment, for the examples following are rarely confessed as grave sins. If the citations disturb the conscience of some, it is well. Note, however, that the following are the *exceptions* to the common experience of most religious.

A "conscience-stricken" religious must expose in detail the failings of others to superiors with the plea that the common good and public propriety and the order's public image is suffering. Except for truly scandalous conduct, a nun who lingers to talk a few times to a young man, a priest who drank too much at two parish affairs, a brother who is testy with long-winded women on the phone, are scarcely deserving of the often-magnified reports given of them. I have noticed that those who regard

us well place a favorable connotation to our actions automatically; those who do not wish us well, a pejorative
meaning.

A second common example is the "justly indignant" superior who wishes only the spiritual progress of the subject. Some disagreement on household policy, even the
venially sinful criticism of the superior, does not constitute rebellious behavior, which a superior has some
vague right to crush and destroy, so that the "broken
spirit will be humbled." What a far cry from the gentle
Christ, who washed his disciples' feet and practically
boasted that he was among them as one who served. The
chapter on relationship of superior and subject will explore this problem in detail. It suffices to say now that a
superior has more temptation to sin mortally through uncharitableness than does a subject.

Undoubtedly the most insidious example of these mortal sins is detraction, which the Sacred Scripture calls the
"abomination of mankind." The detractor differs from a
mere tale-bearer, the first example. This double-tongued
child of Satan generally aims at preventing the promotion of some relatively worthy candidate. I say "relatively," because practically no human being who ever
came to religion to save his soul escaped making at least
a few stupid remarks, acting foolishly and committing
some serious, perhaps greatly sinful, mistakes. The detractor recalls incidents long past, as an outburst of
temper that scandalized some lay persons, indiscreet
views on morality and resentment against some member
of the hierarchy publicly expressed. The suggestion is
brought forward that the "culprit" has not changed,
could not muster the respect of potential subjects, needs
a refresher course in theology—and probably did not

vote for the major superior at the last chapter anyway. The only religious worse than a detractor, who splits the solidarity of the order, is the superior who acts on such ill-advised premises without adequate inquiry. Probably the only time a religious can, after much soul-searching, give such a biographical sketch of a fellow religious or priest without serious detriment to his own soul is at visitation and chapter, when specifically asked. We do not censure the superiors who ask the questions, unless prejudice makes them selective when the answers are evaluated.

St. Paul wrote to the Corinthians, "I hear that there are cliques among you at your meetings. I believe it, since factions must arise, as it were, to make more obvious those of proven worth." The fourth candidate for our rogues' gallery is the divisive person in the community. This religious—more common among women, as the detractor is more common among men—reinforces existing bitterness, urges an offended person to talk back because "it isn't wholesome to bottle up one's feelings," points out the real or inadvertent irritations occasioned by others, has pejorative insights into others' motives. Before long the normal frictions of daily life, generally ignored or even the occasion of merit, have created in a house two camps with convenient labels—progressives versus conservatives, young versus old, Irish versus Polish or German or Italian. Lincoln quoted St. Matthew during the Civil War: "No city or household split by factions can endure."

I indicated in the last four paragraphs that mortal sins of uncharitableness are possible in community life. I repeat, even at that the sketches above represent the exception. Lack of charity as a venial sin shows its colors in hypersensitivity, hostility to correction, flare-ups of temper, criticism of household facilities, imposition of one's own opinion on others, repeatedly using one person as the butt of jokes, insincere flattery, sarcastic observations. Perhaps because charity is the last virtue we seem to acquire, the one most easily lost, the one most tiresome to guard against interiorly, and the one which makes us most like God, it is called the queen of virtues.

When the theologians say that every sin, however individual and interior and private, has a social effect, if only to weaken one's own function in the Mystical Body, the parade example is uncharitableness. I believe we are more likely to rise to heroic charity in great adversity—as in a concentration camp—than in the exigencies of daily monotony. When death is remote, we lose the eschatological viewpoint of life. Hence we remember from the wartime and current prison confinements of religious and priests how they shared meager food in a situation where many had to steal to survive, and how they risked beatings to give spiritual comfort or absolution to fellow prisoners.

I often tell young people who wonder if they are in love about the charity that is the heart of love. Love to most of us covers a multitude of meanings; to the young it conveys the overtones of emotion, even sentimentality, very strongly. It generally includes—and this is not entirely evil—a certain amount of self-seeking and self-enhancement. But charity, as a Christian virtue, energizes human love and perfects it in a particular way. Charity, the "bond of perfection," enables love not to be blind, contrary to the popular saying. Charity sees beyond the present moment of ebullience, of ecstasy, of mutual emotion. *Charity observes and recognizes, then accepts the failings of the beloved.* Charity sees pettiness, possessive-

ness, selfishness, but smiles because of the greater good
of sharing a life together.

The condition of a religious is not unlike the young
person in love. Even when we do not particularly like
another, because of incompatible views on politics or
spiritual writers or whatever, we can overlook these
things—which are not even sins, to be sure—and love
that person disinterestedly (although what is held as
common by reason of our faith and our vocation is in-
calculable). To *like* a person is to find satisfaction or
gratification or pleasure or return; to *love* a person is, for
a religious, to find God operative through him or her.
Persons are vessels of grace and glory, now or potentially.
In practice few people distinguish between this "like"
and "love," but it is true nevertheless. In fact, we are not
guilty of sin just because we do not find ourselves attracted to every co-religious, since our natural tendencies
were established through conditioning of many kinds,
long before our entry into religion. But, I suppose, if we
were more perceptive, we could more easily submerge
nature in super-nature. Hence the ballad singer, who
does not like that her man has "done her wrong," can still
love him without gratification or return. So, too, can the
properly motivated religious, who recognizes that human
love is a spark of the divine fire. This should be the primary motive for charity between religious. As Christ's life
had its greatest immediate impact on the Apostles, so our
Christ-life should have its most enduring effect on our fellow apostles. Nothing makes piety more attractive than
kindliness to those for whom we have no natural attraction. It is sad to see religious gracious to outsiders, but
lacking in understanding to those whom we ought to love
most on earth, members of our spiritual family, with

whom God placed us because his providence foresees eternally the type of persons by whom most expeditiously we are to be sanctified.

Many of the problems and frictions in a community could be resolved, or at least ameliorated, by a little face-to-face dialogue. When we are forced to verbalize our feelings and set down attitudes in terms of specific irritations, we no longer can rationalize our own guilt or magnify that of others. Especially do we suddenly see how childish we have been. To learn to laugh at oneself is among the greater skills of religious life. I suspect most of the uncharitableness of religious is due to a lack of communication, revealing our heartache and what has stuck in our throats, and honestly manifesting our needs. None of this is what the eminent spiritual directors call "fraternal correction," about which theory I have no opinion, as I have never observed it successfully practiced. Probably the only ones who can correct fraternally are those disinclined to do so, and whoever can be so corrected probably does not need it.

Living in the wake of Vatican Council II, we can recall the first ecumenical council of the Church at Jerusalem in the time of the Apostles. It has special impact for religious. Theologians say the Apostles were surely sinless after the descent of the Holy Spirit on Pentecost. St. Peter, having been influenced by Judaizers about circumcision and the celebration of Jewish feasts, was opposed by St. Paul, who did not wish to place such an onus on the Gentiles. Did St. Peter resent St. Paul, a newcomer, as "one born out of due time"? In any event, the fifteenth chapter of the Acts records that a bitter contention arose between these sinless spiritual leaders to the degree that they separated from each other. Was the anger indeliberate and the emotional flare-up still charitable? I do not know. But I do know that the Holy Spirit guides the leaders of the Church, extending to them the grace of office, and provides for the happy net results of the supreme councils of the Mystical Body. We might also remember that Sts. Peter and Paul remained co-apostles of the charity of Christ and died in Rome as martyrs for it.

In a wider meaning of charity between religious, the attitudes existing between orders (and between religious and diocesan clergy) need our scrutiny. I remember reading how the French Recollect Franciscans, for example, had exclusive mission right to the territories of New France in America in the seventeenth century. Yet for the good of souls they helped the Jesuits (who were to write the most glorious page of missionizing there) to circumvent the Huguenots, whose money controlled Canada and the French King. The two communities lived for some time in the same household and shared their experiences. As the saying goes, "One hand washes the other." In missions today the need is so obviously staggering, that cooperation also prevails. But it appears wherever the faith is not under duress—as where individual religious are not under the duress of imprisonment, poverty and persecution—there is some reinforcement of traditional or national rivalries, which are a curse among religious. Competitive recruitment techniques often prevail, as well as the desire to maintain exclusive control of certain schools, parishes, or institutions, to the detriment of the Church at large. The widely current ill-will—although surely still the exception—between religious men and women and the diocesan clergy creates a miserable "public image" of religious. Iconoclasm is in order!

Why does such uncharitableness exist in the macrocosm of the Church or order and in the microcosm of the local community? We can cite the envy of another's talents and success, which implies the envious religious' failure to achieve (since everyone has some area of talent). Among younger religious in particular one can see even the envy of spiritual growth, which makes the weaker person impute hypocrisy to such success. We can cite the pride of some who cannot bear the preferment of others, especially younger members, by superiors. We can cite the spiritual laziness and melancholy that is exposed by comparison with better members; hence that religious fancies that he grows if he can demean others. I believe that most often uncharitableness arises from a generalized laxity, of which the sharp tongue and critical mind is only one expression. We have not identified with Christ, we have not lived the Christ-life, we have not meditated on the rejection Christ experienced, we have not seen Christ in others. Everything in religious life is Christ and Christ and Christ.

6 : On Being Human

St. Francis de Sales wrote a heavy book, *Treatise on the Love of God,* in which he reduced all dogmatic and moral theology to different ways we love God and our neighbor, as the expression of the love of God. Sacred Scripture warns us we are liars if we say we love God, but hate our neighbor, for how can we love God, whom we do not see, if we hate our neighbor, whom we *do* see? Therefore just one chapter cannot have exhausted what needs to be said about loving God as he exists and operates through nature and grace in the souls of our neighbors. Almost the whole last chapter was negative: uncharitableness is how we fail to love. What is the image on the obverse of the coin? How do we *mint* the face of Christ?

Christ is the perfect human being and the possessor of integral humanity. Christians look to the Master to see how to love their neighbor whom they do see. The first requisite of such love is to be yourself, not someone else —that is, do not adopt personality traits, habits, poses, sayings, which do not reflect you. We all tend to adopt the traits of those we admire; the imitation of Christ is exactly this. But we cannot love anyone, even our-selves with the proper perspective, unless we chip away the prejudices that come from thinking too often about ourselves. It is characteristic of young religious that they number daily faults even on paper—I know this is even the custom in some communities. Some suffocate natural-ness by choosing postures and attitudes at prayer, in walking, or at table. Others fancy themselves great spir-itual directors and indulge in serious and edifying con-versations merely as a kind of demonstration of their piety. It is not unusual that tyros do this, but it is unfor-tunate if older religious still indulge this kind of self-centered posturing. After a while it becomes a way of life and a substitute for earthiness—the etymological root of the word, "humility." Accept yourself with failings and limitations; set the goal of holiness as shown you by Christ. Even though your humanity, due to original and personal sin, is not integral like Christ's, at least you can be humble. The person who accepts himself has true love for self, too, because he is freed from worrying about real or supposed slights and about the unrealistic goals in life he cannot attain anyway. Humility is the starting point of being human. The saints searched their souls often enough; who in religion can escape self-scrutiny? But they were too concerned with God and souls to dwell on anything of themselves, except how little they had done in comparison with the graces they had received. Humil-ity as the virtue of self-knowledge and emotional matur-ity will be considered in a later chapter. The point of this chapter is to hurry on to the chief fruit of humility within the community, the positive side of love—not just avoid-ing uncharitableness, but extending yourself as a warm, affectionate, understanding possessor of the Christ-life.

In our own time hagiographers are taking great pains to expose the human side of saints, but it has not had much effect on masters and mistresses of novices, clerics, seminarians, aspirants, postulants. I read one Rule, for example, that required the religious not to turn the head lightly or suddenly, but gravely, only when necessary. Otherwise the religious should look straight ahead, except for inclining the head forward slightly. The eyes ought not to be moved immodestly, nor the forehead and nose wrinkled, nor the lips too tight or too apart, nor the pace too rapid. If such external "serenity" grows from interior calm, it need not be condemned. If it is merely pointed out as desirable, toward which the religious will automatically gravitate, it is not reprehensible. But to make issue over such externalism is pointless and destroys naturalness, that enterprising and engaging quality of the young. It makes them into dull robots. By middle age most religious have ceased to disturb their conscience over minute external deportment—if, indeed, men ever were so troubled. Warm, affectionate, understanding human nature is not to be forced into preconceived moulds. No weight of community custom and tradition should flatten the personality. Our humanity is to be channeled, not victimized. Plutarch observed many centuries ago that great men and women reveal themselves less by the record of their public deeds and noteworthy achievements, than by their jokes, private conduct, letters and expressions, and behavior at home. A boon to all religious is the fact that St. Teresa of Avila wrote many of her letters without thinking of posterity and her possible place in history; nor did she seek to edify for the sake of edification. She thanked the donors for gifts of quinces and butter. She gave nicknames to people of whom she was fond. She was apparently subject to "personality clashes" with other nuns, though not also guilty of sin since it was involuntary. She was kind to the poor, yet angry with unethical businessmen who tried to defraud her. She enjoyed dancing and singing at recreation. She was practical enough to see that her nuns couldn't pray well, if they had to worry where the next meal came from. She could make the meatless meals required by the Rule so appetizing that she was considered a first-rate cook. This is the spirit of a woman who was a mystic and spiritual writer of top quality, and who reached the ecstatic during some moments of prayer. This is the positive side of community charity; this is humanity at work with religion. Not everyone, of course, is as out-going as St. Teresa at recreation, or St. Francis on his deathbed asking Fra Jacopa Settesoli for a dish of marzipan, but no one is prevented from being natural and unaffected. With the new professionalism necessary for religious apostolates today, there is danger of losing simplicity. Maybe the "old-fashioned" nuns were "just workhorses" in some persons' estimation, but I bow to their fundamentalist faith, their unaffected stories of piety to the children, their reverence without flippancy for priests, and their simple understanding of the meaning of obedience. But it is distressing to enter the houses of certain religious and see them formalistic, stilted, distant, cold with religious and lay visitors. What a dour Christianity! No wonder they are not able to garner vocations.

Probably the greatest support and truest love we can give our fellow-religious is the *example of unaffected holiness.* I will not retell at this time the overworked story of St. Francis and a brother walking along so devoutly with thoughtful faces that they delivered the best sermon of example. The point is not to seek to edify, which generally bespeaks pride, but, then again, not to fail to edify, which generally bespeaks a strange discomfort at being what we're supposed to be in the first place.

A second support of love is *companionship*, shown during recreation, outings and special holidays. To shoot a game of pool, to swim together, to watch television and make fun of the commercials, to discuss a book, play, or movie, to take a walk in the woods with a pipe and a friend, to play a duet on a piano may seem like nothing to a casual observer. But religious companionship and recreation, demanded by the Rule, is an art and a skill developed by practice. It is an act of virtue. It is a sign of imperfection, at the very least, to omit this activity of the common life regularly to correct papers, milk the cows, write a sermon, or counsel. Of course, individual hobbies are recreation, too, but some portion of common relaxation should be spent together daily. Superiors of the young learn more about their community attitudes during recreation than in chapel. If a religious prefers always to be alone, it was probably a mistake for him to have entered the common life in the first place. It is difficult to exaggerate the importance of community recreation in making a religious also an integral human being. Superiors of novices should make clear the psychological and spiritual values of recreation and companionship. They are developments of the more basic ability to love and give oneself to another. If the Gospels do not record that Christ took recreation with his Apostles, it is both because the Gospels do not record very much of Christ's life at all, and because the Man of Sorrows, who had perfect foreknowledge, as a divine person, of his agony and death, is not likely to have felt relaxed enough to throw a ball around or see a parade in Jerusalem as his end grew near.

To visit the sick is so obvious a task that it scarcely needs a mention. But we tend to forget those laid up for a longer time outside the household. We conveniently forget those who may be on sick leave due to mental disorder, or on penance due to disobedience or alcoholism or whatever else. Warmth and affection are never so needed as when a member of our spiritual family is down and out either physically or mentally. St. Francis wrote that if a mother loves her physical family, how much more should a religious cherish his spiritual brother? The ancient formula of seeing Christ in our brothers and sisters is not an empty one. Christ said whatever we do to the least of our brothers we do also to him. A charming story is told of one of the saints who was caring for a sick beggar. As the man's feet were being washed, the stigmata suddenly appeared. Unconcernedly going ahead with the task and without looking up, the saint remarked, "Well, it's you after all, Lord!" It required no shifting of mental gears to realize the beggar was Christ. Even if the story is a legend, the attitude of the saint is not a fable.

The *ready availability* of one religious to assist another with studies, projects, assignments, works of charity and duty is another positive aspect of community love. Younger religious like to remain with older ones whom they respect and admire. This is a marvelous chance to form the younger, who is not to be warded off, avoided, or told to get lost someplace else, but slowly taught to think for himself. Everyone needs acceptance by others, especially by the experienced members of any society—just as a teenager really longs to be drawn into the society of adults he questions. The older members must joke a little with them, answer their barrage of questions seriously, and introduce them into the apostolate, neighborhood and practices of the household. I remember a coterie of elderly religious women in a school, into whose midst a much younger sister, but already in perpetual vows, was sent. Unbelievable though this sounds, she was sent regularly out of the recreation room to bed about an hour before the grand dames who were allowed to linger until night prayers and bedtime!

The *Mirror of Perfection* relates a very human story of St. Francis that illustrates how understanding, tactful and generous a person should be to his co-religious. Apparently one of the newest members of the community, desirous of imitating the austere fasting of long-time members, simply could not fall asleep at night. Dizzy with a headache, his lusty, young stomach no doubt growling, the tyro called out, "I am surely dying!" When St. Francis lighted the friary and sought out the famished brother, he took pity on his youth and especially tried to cover his embarrassment. Therefore in the middle of the night St. Francis had a meal prepared, the lamp lit, and the table set for the whole community. Thus the seasoned religious covered the young man's chagrin with charity and probably a few kindly jokes. Afterwards St. Francis pointed out that everyone must study his own nature, because the Lord wants a humble and contrite heart more than a victim.

So great is the current concern of religious superiors for the apparent lack of charity and understanding and the family spirit, that many orders are closing their minor seminaries and postulancies or aspirancies. Some say it is too early to extract the young from the warmth of family life. Others say it is better for the young to get a "taste of life." It is not appropriate now to discuss family relationships or if that "taste of life" is necessarily wise. Does this attitude merely reflect the bitterness of some older religious who felt they were taken too early into religious life, before *they* understood what they were doing? The real point is often forgotten—besides the fact one should go when one is called by God. If the community provides adequate substitutes, warmth and affection and personal idealism and the example of unaffected holiness, there would be no jeopardy of vocation for the person who already felt called in high school. I am not here referring to the training houses of the young where the recruits go home on month-ends and holidays and have visits frequent enough; nor do I refer to the excellent plan of one order which sends trainees home for the junior year of high school to their own local school. These are psychologically sound, yet even they are not enough *unless the young member wants to hurry back* to the warm companionship and fraternal leadership he finds in his spiritual home. Very few young trainees leave their books and desks with much regret, but if they are glad to escape the autocratic regimen and uncompromising schedule and the uninterested leadership and the mechanical routine, then the order is failing to provide the right teachers and environment for the young member to develop emotionally outside his home. The immature and sensitive are not adults, not soldiers, not criminals. If the overall tone of every religious house were more permissive, with natural and spontaneous dialogue, this would become the thinking in the houses of training as well. Once again, we must return to living the Christ-life and being integrally human.

The most delicate aspect of positively-shown charity in

the community is *friendship*. The previous paragraphs underscored the generalized attitudes of loving-kindness, tolerance and generosity. But the love that is at once most dangerous in a community and yet most fruitful of good (and close to God's love of us) is the friendship between individuals. Educators have a technique of deliberately juxtaposing friends in class or on school projects, because they cooperate more closely and accomplish more work. The students themselves help determine this juxtaposition by sociograms. Yet religious superiors and authors seem to take the opposite stand when friendships bud in the community. What can be said of such associations?

When the little boy going to bed told his mother he was afraid of the dark, she replied that God was there with him. "Yes, I know," the child retorted, "but I want someone with skin on!" This story has a profound point. A child needs caresses and manual contacts and the physical reassurance of his security. A much-loved child will grow easily into heterosexual love and wholesome contacts with his own sex. We all crave "someone with skin on," but the religious has to make a positive choice of a skinless God, for even the Incarnate Son, even the Eucharistic Christ, is not present to us in a familiar form. For the immature and young religious, whose spiritual state generally has more emotional overtones than older men and women, there is a real danger that the merely human desire to touch, kiss, hold and embrace may enter. This is a rarity in the friendships of older members. Even for the young the danger is somewhat remote; they seek the reassurance of belonging to someone precisely because a young person is uncomfortable at being left out of any of life's currents. If there is an exchange of small signs of predilection as gifts and affections, there is not necessarily any sin or perversion, but only the clumsy desire to love and be loved in a tangible way, because the young person is generally incapable yet of adult and disinterested friendships. It would be more serious if the friends were to exclude others regularly from their companionship and seek an exclusive liaison. Yet the danger is still more one of divisiveness in the community than sin. A remonstrance from a gentle superior with the rational explanation of mature friendship is the best remedy, but dismissal is the wisest prescription if the exclusiveness continues. We applaud lovers on a honeymoon, for example, that they seek exclusive privacy for their intimacies. But they also learn, as their married love matures, that both husband and wife need contacts with many others—children, friends, relatives, neighbors, business associates—to integrate themselves with the daily world.

This so-called "particular friendship" is usually a transitory thing. What about legitimate affection between religious? The Book of Sirach calls a faithful friend a strong shelter, a treasure of priceless value, and a life-saving remedy, for both will aid each other in the fear of the Lord. Elsewhere it is written that a brother who helps a brother is like a mighty fortress, impregnable to enemies. Christ had special friends among the Apostles, Peter, James, and Andrew. To his best friend, John, he committed the care of his mother. There were men and women —like laymen today—who did not follow Christ everywhere as the Apostles, but, as disciples, stayed with him when he was in their area, to minister to him. And we know he sought refuge and relaxation with Mary, Martha and Lazarus from time to time. He even wept when

Lazarus died, although he knew he was going to raise him again to life.

One might reason that Christ was such an integral person, without our proclivities, that his love was always properly ordered to his mission. Yet the saints were like Christ in their special friendships. Sts. Benedict and Scholastica were friends as well as brother and sister. Sts. Basil and Gregory Nazianzen were school-chums, who grew into scholar-friends for life. Sts. John of the Cross and Teresa of Avila used to tease and nickname each other. St. Thomas Aquinas once wrote to a friend that he set aside his prayers to write him. Sts. Francis and Clare were intimates, and when he died, she so mourned the loss of her spiritual director that they brought his body to San Damiano so she could look upon him from her cloister window for the last time. The Little Flower was hailed by her co-religious as the spark-plug of recreation period because of her warmth and gaiety. Therefore it is hard to understand the pejorative attitude of so many spiritual directors and writers who say a friend is merely a crutch and "the only friend of a religious is Christ." Is it possible that such authors are more perfect than Christ and the saints, or that they were themselves the victim of an evil friendship, or that they were exaggerating, or only that they never learned how to love a friend in God?

Sisters particularly complain that they are suspect if seen in the same company too often; they say they cannot find the humanity and natural friendships they knew and profited from before religious life. They sometimes conclude they are inferior religious. Because men have greater mobility and opportunity of outside contacts, they seldom feel this stricture in religious life, particularly because men are less demonstrative. But priests who direct nuns ought not overlook their need for natural love, upon which supernatural love can build. The greater sensitivity a religious has to natural love—a desirable trait—the greater is his or her potential for divine love. Just as in every family some cousins or even brothers and sisters are closer than the rest, so in the religious state. "By their fruits you shall recognize" spiritual friendships —serenity, mutual cheer, support, a "sounding board" against which to discuss our opinions and interests. If the fruit is gossiping, sharing of stupid secrets, argumentativeness, and complaining, re-examination of the friendship is in order. A mature friendship in a community, however, is the best substitute for a sinful liaison outside it. It prevents the seeking of refuge in alcohol or "nervous breakdowns." One cannot decide to "make friends." It happens by itself, or it is a belabored counterfeit that is merely seeking diversion. Pray for your friends; God saw your need and supplied it. Be approachable to all, but give love true human expression in friendship. Perhaps affection for a human friend is the only way some religious will never learn how to be affectionate to God.

7 : The Service of Love: Authority

THE VOWS and all the virtues contingent upon them are facets of the love of Christ—his love for us in giving the example, and our love in following it. Poverty divests itself of things to concentrate on loving their Creator; chastity deprives itself of persons to love the Divine Persons. When I refer to obedience as the service of love, I mean it as a two-way street. The subject serves God through fulfilling an apostolate directed by the superiors of the order. The superior serves God by fulfilling the needs of the subjects, in so far as they are apostles, by making it easier for them to concentrate on divine matters directly. The subjects are freed of administrative detail, troubling over fewer material considerations, and without time-consuming anxiety over contacts with laymen for merely business reasons. I think it was St. Bonaventure who noted that superiors are, therefore, the masters of their subjects in spiritual affairs, but servants of their subjects in temporal affairs.

I have always conceived the history of man on every level of human activity as the collective attempt to return to Paradise. Perhaps the millennium of the Apocalypse will simply dawn gradually with man's perfectibility slowly actualized. Even if the last statement is not true, the attempt to return to Eden is verifiable. On the physical level, medicine attempts to restore the freedom which Adam had from sickness; some scientists speak of indefinite or at least prolonged physical life—and we recall that Adam had the capability of not dying before his fall. On the intellectual level, educators attempt to teach the fit, as well as the exceptional person, whatever he can learn of truth, of occupational skills, of history, of poetry, of art—and we remember that Adam had infused knowledge in the Garden and imagination to catalog all the creatures by name. In fact, so vast is the world's storehouse of facts in libraries and from computers, that it is no longer possible for anyone to be an encyclopedist. On the occupational level, technologists attempt to make labor easier, yet more productive—and we recollect that Adam tilled the Garden and dressed the vines with joy, and that all the animals were domesticated when he walked with God. On the social level, government and social agencies attempt to destroy poverty, establish universal peace and justice by law and persuasion, and balance the haves and have-nots—and we read that Adam's sojourn in Paradise was idyllic and plentiful. The history of man's rise in all these fields of endeavor reveals excesses and deficiencies—as socialism in the field of government and libertinism in art.

But our ultimate restoration to Paradise, both collective and individual, requires the integration of ethics and spiritual life. Adam's ethical and spiritual life was supernatural, hence only Christ, the new Adam, could be the source of supernatural grace, which is a share in divinity. Only by baptism into Christ-life does a human being make himself capable of such integration. What ethical element, then, is the critical point in man's restoration into Paradise? Adam's sin was like Lucifer's—"I will not serve." Occasioned by pride, man's fall was by disobedience. Every Christian must commit himself to obedience to God's law and the precepts of ecclesiastical authority. But a religious stands within the flow of humanity as a rallying point of obedience and a witness to its meaning in the new Paradise of supernatural grace. Specifically in baptism the receiver of the sacrament renounces Satan, his pomp and his works, by which man first lost his kingdom. The religious at profession goes farther and renounces his own will in a service of love. Equally important and mostly forgotten is the fact that the superiors promise a service of love, too, when they assume office— to act as God in Paradise, who walked with the sons of men to forbid and to command, but even more to teach, to explain, to draw to himself by love.

How does the superior fulfill in a practical way the covenant of love the religious community makes with the subject? More obviously we know what a true superior is not, because God is not—domineering, unforgiving, without mercy, lacking understanding, mistrusting, and unsolicitous. Like the best of educators, who accepts an educable person at his real stage of intellectual development and continues the training as individually as possible, so the best of superiors accepts the willing subject at his stage of spiritual development and continues the formation as individually as possible. Justice to all of one's subjects, therefore, does not mean treating everyone the same, as if he were a measurable quantity, but in handling and leading them to the degree and proportion demanded by each person's quality of spiritual life. So delicate a skill is this that not one religious in a hundred is naturally fit to be a superior. But anyone can strive to be less unfit by prayer and practical rules-of-thumb. Take some of the following:

A superior should always assume the subject is basically tractable and reasonable, able to be adapted and fundamentally an idealist. I never saw a newly-professed or a newly-ordained member of any community to whom such a description did not originally apply. The role of the superior in reinforcing those who are still idealistic and restoring those who are not, is to give them something to which to rise and a standard of excellence by which to measure themselves. As in the previous chapter, the greatest charity between religious is that of good example. There cannot be two standards of freedom, of acquisition of personal objects, of hobbies and collections, of libraries, of automobiles, of money for individual uses, of conveniences (I do not even mention luxuries) in one's rooms and offices and places of work, of recreation, of access to lay persons, of disposition of free and work time. There would be little eagerness for most subjects to become superiors except for the frequently prevailing double standards between superior and subject. The slight prestige and freedom would never outweigh the headaches of being a businessman outside the house and an umpire inside. St. Theresa of Avila notwithstanding, I believe a holy man ultimately means more to the community than a good administrator, because a truly holy man would never be unfair, morose, mistrustful and closed to suggestion.

St. Francis was always worried about his chief role as exemplar to his young fraternity. When the stigmata and other physical ills made a fur-lined garment necessary, he insisted the fur be placed on the outside, lest he receive adulation from his confreres for a mortification he was not exercising. At another time St. Francis took temporary residence in a tower of the palace of Cardinal Leo and was tormented by temptations the very first night. He allowed that the spiritual torments were occasioned by his relatively superior lodging, when his friars were living in wattle huts and suffering in mission territories. There was no compromise in the example given by the "Christ of Umbria."

I said the prudent superior accepts the subject with whatever spiritual quality he manifests. He does not break the bough or quench the burning flax by intolerable pressures. Everyone has eccentricities of some sort and ethical opinions that are bound to nettle one's co-religious. Not only does the superior overlook what is merely a sinless type of self-expression, however irritating to others, but also the superior does not foist his own eccentricities on his subjects—say about the length or need of vacations, the artistic value of avant-garde films, the spiritual profit of contact with lay persons, the seeking of benefactors, or other policies and opinions neither actually determined by the Constitutions nor related to sin. Sometimes a relaxation of the rules in favor of a human weakness is even in order, saving matters of sin.

Anent the importance of giving the subject a goal to strive for and a standard by which to measure himself, the wise superior learns to delegate his authority freely. He says to the subject, "This will be your contribution to the community. Give me periodic reports, but the right to make on-the-spot decisions is yours in this circumscribed area of competence. Just stay within what you know the general policies of the community (institution, parish) are." Instead of misinterpreting the zeal of young members as ambition, and their energies as a criticism of himself, the superior should realize all effective apostolates redound to the good of the Church and order and the good reputation of the household. Individuals never rise and fall alone in a community; a mark of approval or shame is stamped on the *collective* personality. As for older subjects, they need the feeling of being trusted, of being asked their advice, of being delegated without minute supervision to run the bursar's office, the youth club, the altar society, the school pep club, the drama circle, the C. F. M., the catechetical series, the community benefit and ticket sales, the building program, the liturgical revival, and so on. The knowledge of being trusted helps to make one trustworthy, as the knowledge of being loved helps to make one loving.

At community councils and house chapters, the superior should extend knowledge of common enterprises and share the yet-unpublished movements and transfers, once they are not secret anymore. One area of serious neglect may be cited here. The major superiors tend to inform only a select group about the advances or setbacks of the province. Further, those in training are seldom made aware of the achievements and projects, troubles and sorrows of the province. In both cases cited, the rank and file are made to feel they have no stake in the community, that they are second-class citizens, that they are not important enough to add their enthusiasm in prosperity and their prayers in adversity. As for the superiors who do not consult their subjects on notable expenditures, who make their life intolerable, or pursue new projects without advice, there is no recourse beyond canonical visitation and patient suffering as a "victim soul" for the community.

Naturally the superior must correct, especially if he or she has delegated someone authority and has given them the chance for self-expression and individual responsibility. The fact that a superior does *not* have to correct may be due less to wise administration than autocratic domination, a rigid horarium and the lack of opportunity for the subject to choose to do anything for himself in the first place. A correction, however, is not the same as punishment. It is like a hypodermic of a physician: the solution is carefully mixed, the skin is cauterized against inflammation, and the needle is administered as quickly and painlessly as possible by a deft hand. St. Francis reminded the superiors in the rule that "anger and perturbation inhibit charity in themselves and others." While the superior should not prevent a subject from explaining if his good name or a major wrong were involved (not in the case of small infractions or obvious ones) nevertheless the superior should also hope and pray that the subject does not to try to justify himself.

A hard superior who is unapproachable, irascible, or curt is the worst cross of any religious house. Such a person does more to destroy vocations, disturb the peace of soul, deprive the needy or sick of material aid, lower the dignity of the religious and fracture family unity than a thousand devils tempting the members. Such hardness and unapproachability is devilish, because it is the antithesis of the fatherly God, the gentle Jesus, the forgiving Spirit of Love. Such hardness excludes charity at the top, from whence all good should filter down into the community, and it cripples apostolic progress for want of Christ-like leadership. The sick are embarrassed to ask for medicine or a visit to a doctor, optometrist, or dentist, because of the grudging consent. Those religious who need a special confessor or psychiatric help fear to approach the superior on such a delicate matter, which worsens their problem. Such superiors are one of the chief means God permits to chastise a religious house. No one wants a superior to coddle a revolutionary, to permit scandalous behavior, to countenance divisive forces in the house, but, then, no one wants to live in a household where artificial conformity reduces the human beings to a row of mediocre, visionless, thwarted robots. St. Philip Neri, though a superior and religious founder, never commanded his subjects anything outright, it is said. He prefaced his orders by a "please" and "if you don't mind." Particularly he asked a subject up for a change, "If I were to send you out on this assignment, would you go willingly?" There is no record that St. Philip's subjects were recalcitrant, unmanageable, or unresponsive.

One generality put forth at the start of this chapter could be explained adequately only in a book—that the superior, who is the servant in temporal matters, is the master in spiritual things. Of all the virtues that spiritual authors make serve as a summary of the spiritual life, the spirit of prayer is what the superior should look to foster in the community. Prayer means *contact* with God, the uplifting of the earthbound to heaven. Therefore the superior needs to provide blocks of time for true contact with God and to beware of imposing too many tasks, so the spirit is submerged by the temporalities of a particular apostolate. Our vocal prayers do not necessarily give us contact with God; they are often said when we are dead tired in the morning or evening (or right after a busy day in school, as some sisters deplore). No schedule can please everyone, since our prayer life is so conditioned by *natural* habits. The subjects should be reasonable. But every person needs free time to think out problems.

Brothers and sisters busy with manual labor are less likely to see the apostolic overtones of their work than teachers, preachers, administrators and those busy with intellectual work in general. Therefore, not only must the superior keep pointing out the expiatory and supplementary nature of their work to them, but also provide the time for them to be "busily idle," that is, to read, to walk about, to study, to think, to feed their ideals with the wholesome daydreams that lead to action and self-determination. One religious deplored the fact her superior always invented some extra chore when she was seen with a book in the library. It is a pity that a superior is more interested in clean floors than clean souls. What a wonderful system that grants a "sabbatical" leave from time to time—especially when the effect of profession or ordination wears off—for the religious to find a holy mountain on which to sit for a couple months and read all the spiritual books he meant to for the last ten years. The religious who are too busy or disinclined to look for a mountain need to be sent all the more.

Many of the demands of authority are relics of the past, rather than mere needling or peevishness. The superiors, especially of women, were trained to make these demands by custom or law, which are merely the vehicles of foolish traditions and often empty exhibitionism. Pope Pius XII warned, "The customs of religious that are only external or of historical value can even hinder the greater good." I am not saying that foolish democracy or excessive social freedom should color religious obedience. But neither democracy nor social freedom are evil in themselves, and we are the children of our times. Since candidates to religious life can enter recent or modernized religious orders, or lay religious groups, in which medievalism for its own sake was never an issue, the other type of order might just as well close down as operate expensive training houses for a decreasing number of vocations. I remember a cold and formalistic nun, whom other members of the community had continually to justify before disgruntled lay persons and her students, on the grounds "she is a good religious and observes all the rules so literally we call her the 'living rule'."

What are some examples of either degrading, pointless, or just plain silly demands of the kind just brought up? In one community the nuns must assemble regularly and *ask permission to ask permission* to carry out the assignments *already* given them or to do such obvious things as wash and dress and read. What a waste of precious time! In another community a pencil stub may not be thrown away unless the superior decides it has been used long enough; in another, the same is true of a piece of thread even four inches long. In another community the subject is not allowed to choose her own book of spiritual reading without supervision. The list is embarrassingly long and detailed; practically every community has some such burdens. The implication is that an adult is too wasteful or childish or stupid to know when to discard pencils and thread, or how to choose a spiritual book intelligently. Some loyally counter it is an act of humility and a means of increasing one's merit. It may be true in individual cases, but I am not yet convinced that the sense of responsibility so dulled by fatuous dependence is sharp enough to distinguish mortal and venial sin, make wise choices, correct students' papers prudently, and so on. In crowded conventual timetables, one must use the quickest ways of becoming an integral person of maturity sufficient for grace to build upon. One gets so bogged down in endless details and strictures and customs that one forgets the maxim of St. Augustine, "Ama et fac quod vis"— "Be a lover and you can do as you please," which is the same as to say, "Anyone who loves enough is inspired enough to detach himself effectively from creatures, so as to belong to the Creator." The service of love of authority ceases to be service or love, if authority places more stumbling-blocks to sanctity than the world, and flesh, and the devil have already set for a religious.

Enough! Let us reverse the coin of authority and note the qualities of that love of service called obedience.

8 : The Love of Service: Obedience

THE RESTORATION of Paradise begins on the moral level with the right ordering of the will. It is the imitation of the new Adam, Christ, who leads us back to Eden. It is comparatively the hardest level on which to re-enter Paradise, because we need surrender nothing to regain social, physical, and occupational integrity. But to surrender one's own will and place it at the disposition of even his inferiors requires no small victory over self. After all, we do not lack for necessities and reasonable comfort, and we hopefully trust that the fires of passion will die out in time, but we sense that obedience will get more difficult as we increase in age, experience, and possibly prestige.

It is a wondrous thing to remember what God has done for those who rely on his will. The martyr, St. John de Brebeuf, was one of fifty Jesuits who asked to go to New France as a missionary. He had had such poor health that he was ordained before the regular time, inasmuch as the superiors thought he was near death from tuberculosis. When he was sent to Canada he was a priest for only three years, without his tertianship done, without final vows. He was going to a harsh climate with exhausting winters where no medical help would be at hand. Yet he was one of the five chosen against all odds, because God was subtly arranging events through the superiors on earth. The seed has to die before it can bear fruit.

In chapter fifteen of the First Book of Kings, Saul was commanded by God to smite Amalec and destroy every human and beast. Saul's obedience had some reservations he thought justifiable. He spared King Agag of Amalec and kept the best flocks and garments, not for selfish reasons, but to offer holocausts to God. Samuel was told by the Lord that he regretted having had anointed Saul because of this disobedience. Samuel in turn informed Saul that God preferred obedience to holocausts, victims, sacrifices and the fat of rams; and that God rejected Saul from the kingship. Religious who decide how they shall serve God and improve on the divine mandate may lose the kingdom of heaven. Above all, religious today need a return to fundamental obedience. We are seeing some orders make progress in the Church, because of their movements towards greater democracy and sharing of responsibility. These movements are truly long overdue, but in the final analysis a superior, even a bungling, irresolute and ignorant superior, has the obligation to decide and to command, and the grace of office to see him through. We shall witness the greatest renewal and rejuvenation in those communities where obedience is prized most highly.

St. Francis de Sales says of obedience, "It is definite that we all have a limitless ability to obey, but perhaps no ability at all to command." Many times we hear the dictum that never can be repeated enough: "No one ever lost his soul through obedience," although, as the previous chapter took pains to underline, the excessive demands of authority can *jeopardize* a vocation. Only the authority of God is the proper motive of our service of love. If we look only to the orders, and not to him who gives them, whether we agree or not is secondary.

Our generation is in an anomalous position. In a school we train our students to be aggressive on the athletic field, outspoken in student government, involved in debate and public affairs, and challenging in the classroom —at least such is the desirable mutual attitude between teachers and students. This attitude has arisen not merely from social upheavals of lower classes desiring their just equality with the upper classes, but even more from the need in our scientific and technological age to distrust the techniques and operational skills of the last generation, if we wish to improve society. When the most active and successful students enter a community, especially if under the tutelage of the same order which trained them in grade school or high school, they naturally assume that progress demands further challenge and dialogue. Such questioning minds are actually an asset to the order. It does no good to call the young "the new breed" contemptuously or say, "You have come to religion to listen, not to ask." The skillful leaders of the young will be patient and explain, understanding that such challenges are not meant to be hypercritical, however clumsily phrased, but represent the desire to become a saint as early as possible. The young want to identify closely with the community, hence their actions are searching. Ultimately, however, they must, out of that same challenge and that same conviction, decide to accept the norms established in the order. A parade example is the query of religious about the validity of censoring the mail of the young. This is how I would typically answer the challenge:

"Experience shows that many parents write to their children in religious houses of training about trouble at home, or how much the family misses them. This makes the distant son or daughter feel helpless and weakens the vocation by his remembering the happy times and freedom of which he is deprived in religious life, especially during the early days of training, when loneliness and sentimentalism are 'occupational hazards' I know of another case (I would continue) when immature religious wrote foolishly of their personal spiritual life, or of their occasional depressions, unsettling their family in turn. Another, anxious to recruit vocations, wrote an encouraging letter to someone already considered negatively by the superiors. A male religious wished to write to his previous girl friends; a female religious to one dismissed from the community, towards whom she had felt a special friendship. Another wrote such a poor letter to a potential candidate assigned to him for correspondence that the parents said they would not permit their boy to enter a community if that was the example of intelligence or public relations. I believe older religious should be free of censorship—and most male religious are, at least. But the superior never loses the right to censor mail if there is some suspicion of evil. Still, it is so easy for most religious to mail letters secretly there is no practical effect in censorship in the case of lax religious, just as there is no need of censorship in the case of devout religious. When everything has been said about censorship (I would conclude my instruction), if that is the rule of the institute, you will have to submit—graciously, I hope—to what you cannot change, and wait until you are in a position to alter the rule lawfully. By the time your views may even change!"

In all matters of obedience, mere performance of the required task is not enough. Christ said in the Garden, "Not my will, but yours be done," to his heavenly Father. Thus Christ substituted God's will for his natural inclinations. So the religious must give *interior* assent and *learn*, for this is an acquired skill, that such is God's intention for us at this particular moment, even though he is aware that the superior is objectively in error, is acting in ignorance, or is motivated by prejudice. Now interior assent refers to hearing God's voice in that of a superior; it does not mean we can twist nature, so that we no longer feel a revulsion to our task, or that we can close our eyes to the foolishness or imprudence of a command. When the saints claimed they were dead to such emotions, it was not an exaggeration; they truly heard God's voice in the superior's, and they concluded their own complaints were trivial and weak within the sound of that mighty voice.

Remember, however, the danger of setting up the saints' ideals as a continual theme for yourself, if you are a young religious. Take the grade-school children who hear daily stories of the excessive mortifications, common miracles, pious phrases and gruesome martyrdoms of the saints. They subconsciously reject what they know is unattainable, and thus potential saints are cut off at the roots for want of prudent cultivation. Likewise the young religious and recently ordained priest must accept himself as he is really and understand that ideal sanctity is still far off. Such sentiments, especially with regard to obedience, do not excuse us from perfection, but destroy at once both our pretensions and our discouragements. Even Christ, we read, grew in wisdom and age and grace. By thirty years of childhood and adolescent obedience, he readied himself for martyrdom. I do not say Christ would have been incapable of his agony and passion and crucifixion at the age of twelve; I merely point out that in Gethsemani he asked momentarily that the cup of suffering pass him by, and on Calvary he momentarily sensed his hesitation and his understandable human despair. Thus the perfection of our obedience, Christ is telling us implicitly, consists in our greater willingness to perform our superior's will, but not necessarily in our greater ability to agree with the command or be overjoyed at what is distasteful! I am somewhat suspicious of the psychological state and emotional maturity of the ancient hermits of the legends who were unhappy religious unless someone was thwarting them or at least giving them detailed commands of how to execute infinitesimal details of life. A later chapter will examine this type of spiritual reading.

Now I must bring up the critical topic of *blind obedience*. Like particular friendships, it is a very moot point in our lives. By way of antecedents, I have mentioned the necessity of not compromising obedience if you are sincere in living the Christ-life. Yet even Christ, it seems, did nothing out of blind obedience as many religious understand that phrase, insofar as he had *perfect foreknowledge* and understanding of every salvific act. I also mentioned the dangers of "humble disobedience" and passive resistance to authority. I remember one major seminary where, only a short time before ordination, the seminarians "sat in" the chapel during lunchtime as a demonstration against seminary policies. I know some religious who defy Church authority on grounds of their conscience and urge lay persons to manifest civil disobedience to

public laws in order to make known their political griev-
ances. I have heard of priests who tell their superiors they
cannot abide by the Church's stand on moral issues in the
confessional. I have seen religious brothers who defy a
superior or dare him to get a dispensation for them. Such
religious put Macchiavelli to shame by their plots. One's
conscience must always be safeguarded, of course. The
catechism of vows does speak of only what is rational and
consonant with human dignity as being the object of
vows, human dignity and our *rationabile obsequium*
tending oneself beyond the minimal requirement of the
vows, human dignity and our "rationabile obsequium"
are somewhat ephemeral in defining. What do some of
the spiritual writers claim are examples of blind obedience?

St. Francis, *it is said*, ordered a novice to plant cabbages upside down with the roots sticking out of the
ground. When the novice planted them the right way, St.
Francis was supposed to have sent him home at once
with the remark that he had come to learn and obey, not
to do his own will. If this story is true, the cabbages may
only have been the last act of many disobediences, or
perhaps a test the saint was trying. To be sure, very few
sane men would care to belong to a community where
such testing or ridiculous commands were *customary* or
habitual. And it is one thing when St. Francis told Bernard of Quintavalle to ride backward on an ass through
the town where once he had been a respected lawyer, but
we cannot condone or even believe that St. Francis ordered a friar to walk stark naked through a town to test
his humility. I remember a friar of modern times with a
heart condition who was told to put his finger into an
electric socket to test whether it was alive. I read of an

ancient hermit who was commanded by his superior to walk into the Nile River where crocodiles abounded. I recall the story of the nun, made into a movie, in which the nun was told to fail an examination in college deliberately, so another sister might be somehow placated. The nun, unable to do this, always felt she was unfit for the religious state, because she lacked blind obedience. As a matter of fact, any competent spiritual director would point out that to fail the test would have been to perpetrate a lie, since a test is supposed to gauge the extent of one's knowledge. No doubt those commands contrary to safety, morality or human dignity, however, are a rarity and do not merit prolonged consideration.

Blind obedience, as I see it, consists of acting without trying to discern or judge the *superior's* reasons. In that sense blindness is the proper quality of obedience. However, how will subjects, especially young subjects, ever *learn* how to be wise superiors themselves, if the reasons for decisions are never told them? If a subject *inquires* the reasons, particularly for the peace of his conscience, it is right to tell him; if the subject *demands* the reasons or makes his obedience *contingent* on the reasons, it is not right to tell him. But when a superior is about to command a subject to accept a transfer or assign him to a new, sizeable task, sound psychology would urge a discussion beforehand. Is it a necessity? Of course not; religious orders have functioned for sixteen hundred years without such discussions. Why now? Democracy and challenge again? No. In the past, religious did not need specialized training to run farms, copy books, isolate themselves in monasteries, preach the gospel to simple folk and so on. The skills of religious life were few and often learned, as domestic and agrarian chores, before monks and friars and nuns entered the community. It was at this time that most of the maxims and principles of the religious state were formulated. Today's apostolates are varied, technical and require even years of training. Whereas it required only a little shift for a medieval monk to exchange a milk pail for a plow at the superior's command, or a copyist's desk for a bookkeeper's, or one friary for another, or the sewing room for scullery, nowadays we need master's degrees in particular teaching areas, experience in cooking for modern palates in push-button kitchens, theological training to be effective in catechetics, time to practice art and music to become expert enough to communicate, a background of pulpit and confessional experience to be a home missionary, training in language and mores to be a foreign missionary. Can a superior, especially of a whole province, be so naive as to expect to know everyone's background and proclivities from a file cabinet and move the members like chessmen? Is a superior unaware of the basic approach to our departmentalized life by which childhood conditioning or natural bents and talents make a man or woman more successful in one field than another? Does personal enthusiasm count for nothing in an apostolate? After the discussion between a superior and subject, or at least a relevant exchange of carefully written letters, the superior's task is to *decide*, with much prayer and searching of conscience, and the subject's task is to *obey*, with much prayer and searching of conscience. The same is true of house and provincial chapters; the members are required to voice opinions, but once the vote is taken or the decision made, blind obedience, in the good sense, precludes value judgments any more. In this sense, obedience is also charity.

How did every new apostolate begin in religious communities if not by the natural bents of a member who was inspired by a divine enthusiasm to make fresh starts and save souls with different, often startling techniques? I remember the *Frati Volanti*—"flying friars"—of northern Italy, who helped to defeat communists in some of the urban elections by rushing to the places of the communist meetings and challenging the speakers with facts and arguments blasted across the piazza from their own public-address system!

Prior to the strange developments of the religious conscience in our times, when "respectful disobedience" and "humble protest" became status symbols of "progressive" sanctity, blind obedience was not such a widespread issue. It was understood that the perfection of blind obedience was characteristic of the last stages of sanctity, whereas the persons who challenge the concept today are the weak, vacillating beginners. An example of how blind obedience is not the virtue of beginners is St. Therese's approaching the Holy Father to enter Carmel before twenty-one. Her immaturity and religious inexperience were the cause of the petition; I am reluctant to say God inspired her specially to cross the superiors of Carmel after their refusal. I actually think, since few humans have repressed their critical faculty and discretionary ability, that one cannot demand *interiorly* blind obedience—only pray that a subject develops it; and one cannot force himself to give it—only pray that one can suspend his judgments for the love of God. Our love of service grows more profound when our interior sentiments accurately mirror our exteriorly calm and obedient demeanor.

Once again, blind obedience is the virtue that does not

question motives and reasons and prudence of the superior in those matters (practically everything) which he can decide in the disposition of one's time and talents. Whether it is a natural gift, more than an acquired virtue, and possible only by grace, I cannot say. But I doubt if God withholds it from those who ask and try to earn it. How can the gift of blind obedience be earned; is that not a contradiction of terms? All graces are a gift, but *no one receives the higher until he has fruitfully employed the lower forms of obedience.*

Do you think you have troubles as a subject? St. Alphonsus Liguori was excluded from the community he founded for some time, because the Pope believed in his alleged disobedience. St. Bernard of Clairvaux was blamed for the failure of the Third Crusade, although he preached it unwillingly at the order of the Pope. Because of her visions and revelations, the superior and co-religious of St. Margaret Mary used to sprinkle her with holy water thinking her obsessed by the devil. She was unpopular and harassed by the envy of her sisters, yet Our Lord commanded her to be subject in all things. St. Francis Xavier was condemned behind his back to St. Ignatius Loyola for his supposed excesses and strange methods; yet St. Francis read the letter of reproof humbly on his knees. Blessed Mary Crescentia Hoess suffered misinterpretation for years in the community at Kaufbeuren. They taunted her about her penniless family and the fact that the Lutheran mayor paid her dowry at entrance. Her mysticism was attributed to witchcraft, her silence to intractability. She was given scraps from the table to eat and deprived of her cell, so that she lay down on the corridor or in the damp cellar. If it is any consolation, after many years the superior was deposed and

Crescentia herself elected. St. John Baptist de la Salle was once removed from the community he had founded by the Archbishop of Paris. Once he was suspended because the local pastor complained his boys were attending Sunday Mass in St. John Baptist's chapel—but the saint would not tell the Archbishop it was because the boys were so ashamed of their poor clothes and notoriety as "bad boys." In fact, St. John Baptist *died* under this suspension from saying Mass and administering the Sacraments, yet without complaint.

If our problems are not so great, at least remember our graces and opportunities *are* as great. St. Paul wrote to the Ephesians, "Do not serve with the hope of being seen and to win the approval of men, but as the slaves of Christ, who do the will of God with all their heart."

9 : Love: The Base
of the Pyramid

ONE OF THE ancient Roman philosophers made a well-phrased, but startling statement some two thousand years ago and it has plagued religious orders ever since. The medievals, then Thomas à Kempis in the *Imitation of Christ*—truly a spiritual masterpiece—would quote, "Every time I go out among men, I come back less a man." If any religious of the twentieth century come back less a man or woman of God, probably that person went out with less than a religious purpose.

Tracing the evolution of religious orders discloses some relevance to this packed phrase. The hermits were living a Christ-life in explicit defiance of the pagan cities, and their whole point was isolation and solitude. The only models of their religious state, newly-arisen in Christendom, were the schools of the prophets who trumpeted God's messages out of the wilderness. Yet many of these ancient men and women supported themselves by their labors, such as weaving cloth or making baskets to be sold to city people. The general impermanence of such groups and the relative dearth of such vocations in the Church for many centuries underline the fact that the eremitical life is an important, but limited expression of the desire for the religious state. The value of those rugged men and women to the history of the religious life is to manifest the importance of breaking with past environment, isolating oneself from distracting occupations and secluding oneself with God as companion. The very idiosyncrasies and exaggerations of that trend in religious life quickly pointed to the need for authority and organization.

First in the Near East, then in southern Europe, men and women grouped themselves into monasteries around which villages developed. It would have been somewhat like kicking a dead dog for a medieval monk to protest that going out among men dulled his spiritual acuity. What would he or she have done in a little village, or even, in later centuries, in a larger town, dressed as they were in an identifiable garb? If it were a question of the occasion of sin, there would have been enough in the monastery from one's own fallen nature. If the trappings of the wealthy or the "luxuries" available at a fair or market were an occasion of envy or distraction, it is not saying much for the quality of their religious life. In the main the monks had a far more secure, orderly and well-provisioned life than most Europeans of those days. But these admirable preservers of civilization taught religious for all time the value of *united* striving for perfection, of *mutual* support in their apostolate, and of having a purposeful goal and tangible direction. The results benefited the whole Church, not just themselves.

To save souls, you have to go where the souls are. When towns grew and local governments became secularistic, the communities of friars were added to the general trends already evident in the religious state. They

bore witness to the Gospel by living its counsels outside
the isolation of monasteries. They, and their female coun-
terparts where appropriate, went into hospitals and
leprosaria, into universities where the monks could not
reach, into mission lands or specialized apostolates where
a large monastery could not readily be planted. Their
essential mobility aided the current spiritual need of the
Church to have someone give the example of the Christ-
life to those who did not live anymore in the shadow of a
monastery; their example was also the more immediate
for appearing more like Christ's. This example of voluntary poverty and detachment, often coupled with profound learning and special skills—as of the classroom and
pulpit, added new features to the face of religion which it
has retained into modern times.

Whether these orders lost their evangelical appearance
or were swallowed up in the complex accretions of organization and large houses, which resembled monasteries
again, is a matter for historians to ponder. It was probably a combination of both. In any event there were apparently no "shock troops" or sufficient visible examples
of the vitality of the Gospel to counteract the reformers'
charges against the Church. No doubt there were holy
souls even in the later-Protestant countries, but is is obvious they had lost contact with the rank and file of Christianity, otherwise the Reformation would either have
failed or been unnecessary in the first place. If the friars
and mendicants of the High Middle Ages until the early
Renaissance went out among men and their orders survived and thrived, they and the thousands of women
religious, who arose in those centuries to carry on caritative works, were not coming back less of a man or
woman. If there were defections, we must remember

there will always be defections. If there was a decrease in the religious spirit, may we not in part attribute that also to the decrease in face-to-face apostolic contacts? Do we not in the modern religious orders, which are suffering from a lack of vocations, have a rather smug and formalistic and isolationist view of the apostolate in which we, both men and women, dispense our spiritual goods largely to those who make themselves available and look upon the laity as beneficiaries of our largesse?

The post-Reformation orders, like all new foundations, grew apace according to the initial apostolic impetus of the founders. In time they also became just diocesan priests disguised as religious, and the women became just other institutes in the Church, but with the titles of newer mysteries of Our Lord and Our Lady. I believe the proper interpretation of the ancient dictum is that when a religious order has already lost its apostolic viewpoint and religious fervor inside the community, then it is dangerous to go out among men without safeguards. As I said in an earlier chapter, renewal starts with houses of training.

There is a wonderful upsurge today of new religious groups in the Church, called *lay religious*, in so far as they live an individual life of vows or promises without the support of a religious house. Some return periodically to a house of training for revitalization or even live in daily community, but work as lay persons at ordinary occupations, living an apostolic Christ-life by the probity of their example. These experiments attest to the spiritual flexibility of the religious state. They point out not only that going out among men need not mean coming back less a spiritual man or woman, but also that the existing orders need such a face-lifting again. There is a need in the contemporary Church for renewal, revival and re-evaluation of the apostolic zeal of religious founders, rather than the multiplication of new communities in the Church. Religious must go out among men in order to leave them more sanctified. I suppose, if the world lasts long enough, after the present mandate of the Church to religious institutes to revitalize themselves has worn itself out, another council, another world heresy, another rash of religious founders, another series of crises, like war and famine and epidemic, will give rise to another re-newal and up-dating.

The foregoing paragraphs, despite their bald generali-zations about history, may serve to place the following paragraphs into perspective. The last few chapters were all about love, both the natural kind necessary for human integrity and the supernatural kind necessary for divine vitality. I pointed out that the love of God expresses itself in the love of neighbor, upon which I touched in general. One's neighbor is first of all his co-religious, hence I talked of charity to all within the community and be-tween communities. Finally I spoke of demonstrating love by authority of the superiors and, conversely, by the obedience of subjects—all under the general title of *serv-ice* to each other in order to serve the Church. But in so far as every baptized person is an apostle and every reli-gious must give adequate testimony of his Christ-life, service from the vow of obedience is also related to souls outside the local household. This seems too obvious to mention to religious occupied in teaching, preaching, nursing, and specializing. Yet an adequate appreciation of the role of religious—as well as diocesan priests in the present context—in the general mission of the Church is well expressed in the structure of an ancient pyramid.

The Church, while it is trying to decrease its spiritual distance from non-Catholics, is essentially missionary. Evangelization means more than recruitment for foreign lands or priest-poor areas at home. The quality of missionary" is applicable to any activity that implements the Christ-life among us anywhere in the world. This is the meaning of the chapter's title, that love is the base of the pyramid. We cannot think of religious and priests as the pinnacle of the structure or the top of the heap. On the contrary, the weakest, least Christian soul in the world is on the top. The deeply-convinced and dedicated lovers of God are on the bottom. Let us hope that religious and priests are the very base and foundation, even as Christ is the cornerstone, of the world's commitment to God. We religious like to think that the laity or non-Catholics exist, at least in some sense, to support us. We rather exist in the Church to support them. The anomaly of religious life—and this is always true in the Church—is that some non-religious and non-clerical persons are closer to the cornerstone. It is we who often are out-ranked in the love of God. If this was never so apparent in the Church before, it is because the laymen have never had the opportunity to be so articulate. Religious must stop hating the world and begin loving it, stop demeaning the world by the epithets of worldliness and begin uplifting it, stop retreating from its curses and begin blessing it by our sanctifying presence.

Religious will always need some seclusion to which to return, plus greater isolation at times of training and renewal. But only as they support a heavier load of souls by face-to-face contact can they claim a nobler position in the pyramid of Christian love. These are grand concepts. How are they applied?

We begin to support others where we have the greatest obligation—to our own natural families. Of course we leave our families behind. Of course they are often the first deterrents before we enter and the strongest threats when we train. Of course we need detachment in the spirit of Christ, who said, "Let the dead bury the dead," and "He who does my will is my mother and sister and brother." Yet Christ loved Mary above all and called his cousin, St. John the Baptist, the greatest of the prophets. Christ surely had natural, obviously sinless regard for his own kin. A religious has the prior obligation to love and pray for and apostolically support his or her own family.

This was well understood by that remarkable woman, St. Catherine of Siena, who held the Lord to his promise to save the souls of every member of her large family! When St. Bernard entered religion, he persuaded four of his own brothers to be among the thirty-one friends he took to the monastery. After he founded Clairvaux, his own father and the last of his brothers entered the Cistercian Order as his subjects. St. Scholastica silenced the protest of her brother, St. Benedict, on the occasion of his annual visit. She wished to prolong the spiritual contact, and he reproved her for her attachment and desire to have him break the Rule. So she prayed and received the favor from God instead, for he arranged such a sudden and violent storm that St. Benedict's departure down the mountain had to be delayed another day. After St. Agnes of Assisi had joined her sister, St. Clare, at the Poor Clare Monastery of San Damiano in Assisi, St. Francis sent her subsequently to make foundations in several large cities of Italy. She was only twenty-three when she parted from her sister, and despite the seedbeds of holiness she prepared elsewhere, she was attached enough to send tearful letters back to Assisi from time to time. Shall we accuse all these great saints of laxity and undue attachment to their families?

Except for St. Catherine of Siena, my examples are of sisters and brothers in religious life. But the parallel is maintained by the saints with their families outside religious life. Damien the Leper wrote on one December twenty-first in his diary-letter to his brother, Pamphile, a priest of the community, and to the rest of his family, that he had just received a packet of letters from home. Before he opened them, he made a mortifying half-hour of thanksgiving, but with utter distraction because of his warm, human, natural love for his family. St. Vincent de Paul admitted his close attachment to family and relations after he went home to celebrate Mass in his boyhood haunts. The day he left he did nothing, he wrote, but cry the entire length of the journey back to his assignment. Thereafter he suffered an agony of desire for three months to visit them again, especially because some of them were so poor that they had to receive alms at times to eat.

A most beautiful testimonial to the filial and familial love of religious is recorded in the life of St. Francis. A poor woman, whose two sons were members of the order, complained of her need to the saint. He gave her the book of the Scriptures, which was used at divine services, to sell, and said God would be better praised by the alms to "our mother"—for that is how he addressed every woman whose son was a member of the order. St. Francis realized that the greatest benefactors of a religious order are the parents of the members. Yet foolish superiors dance attendance on benefactors, who merely give some thousands of dollars, while parents of members must ask to see their flesh and blood like suppliant beggars skulking in the corridors.

The love of family is a wholesome contact and normal outlet of sanctifying love. If more visits both from and to one's family were allowed in the orders where it is rare, perhaps parents would not object to the loss of their sons and daughters as keenly. I realize the time of training, the days of recollection and retreat and the orderly quiet of the religious house are sacrosanct. Cloisters should be refuges of the spirit. It is likewise obvious that enclosed communities of men and women may not and should not multiply contacts or visit outside the house. Theirs is a special vocation, the exact purpose of which is to live in seclusion from every, even apostolic, contact. (Of course, even cloistered orders share their holiness with those who come to the grille.) But if anything is obvious about vocations, it is this: the *majority* are sown in families that are edifying and of sound virtue. Unless the religious is himself weak already, surely the environment in which he received his vocation will not be the environment in which he will lose it.

This contact must be controlled and prudently limited; it probably is by distance and cost of travel. Yet never should contact with one's family be held as a privilege; it is a duty. If love of neighbor has any meaning, then love of family stands in first place among lay contacts for religious, too. It is a favor and consolation particularly for parents. The enforced and prolonged separation from sons and daughters in faraway missions is greatly blessed by God, but when merely antiquated rules or parsimony prevent the prudent offices of filial piety, I am not sure of God's blessing. The ease and speed of modern travel permits living in houses of religious if rules require it still. It is an understanding superior who places members of the institute as near as possible to seriously ailing parents, brothers, or sisters.

So much has been written for centuries—and not without foundation—about doting parents inhibiting vocations, about ambitious parents planning brilliant marriages for their offspring, about solicitous parents smuggling in money or forbidden items to their child, and making surreptitious contacts by letter and telephone, that the more numerous proud and cooperative families are forgotten and only seldom rewarded by a visit to or from their own flesh and blood. One would think that the history of communities is a cloak-and-dagger relationship between the natural and the religious family. The trick is to teach religious to make such visits the occasion of their own and the families' spiritual growth, rather than of complaints about the order and relaxation for its own sake. I will not dignify by comment the unscrupulous practice of making the family pay for travel or making a home visit the enforced occasion of selling tickets and chances. May God have mercy on such superiors.

I have read many suggestions about religious increasing their meager contacts—sisters in C.F.M. groups, clerics in parish study clubs, even novices in visits of service to the poor, theological students in dialogues with non-Catholics. In short, they should see both the needs of some souls and the incredible dedication to God of others. I do not think that such religious will come home less a man or woman. Parish parties and socials, not just the daytime bazaar or evening children's play, when the teachers are not accessible, would be enhanced by the parishioners' opportunity to see the religious informally.

Each community has to evaluate these proposals for itself.

It is a strange interpretation of sisters' roles in the spiritual life of a parish and support of weaker Christians by their example to read that the nuns can go out after dark, for example, to conduct a high-school play, but cannot cross the same school yard to attend benediction or the May rosary. Since many of these parochial devotions are duplicated in the convent schedule, would it not be better to change that schedule so that, for example, during May and October, the sisters join the parish for the common recitation of the rosary? That break in routine alone is often a spiritual uplift. It requires no extra time to practice the apostolate of example. It all depends on how willing the religious are to break down artificial barriers of the Rule. Old members of sisters' communities ought not to be forced into all the new apostolic moulds being suggested, but for which their training has not prepared them. Also, contacts should not be multiplied for their own sake when the members may be burdened enough, as in the case of sisters who teach extra catechism to the public-school children; those who attend public universities with many opportunities to radiate their Christianity while getting a degree; and those who do secretarial or census work, in addition to their regular assignments and household chores.

It is the male religious who have more to fear from contacts outside the community. The resources of money and a car are more available. They can travel without clerical garb and so have easy access to objectionable entertainments and can be out late at night without being recognized. These are the religious who are in danger of returning home "less a man." Yet years of observation have proven to me that sound religious men do not place themselves in occasions of sins. For these latter the danger is in succumbing to the demands of those who take a certain prestige in "collecting" priestly or religious friends, or who delight in extracting information from them about the parish or institution. Sisters do not realize often how fortunate they are to be able to say their rules prohibit such visits.

The gentle St. Francis de Sales gives us a general object-lesson about being human in our contacts with others. He permitted his picture to be reproduced and passed around to his friends, who were importuning him. When criticized for this apparent vanity and attachment to his friends, the saint replied no more harm is done by that small gift of a picture than sharing one's thoughts with his neighbor—and if it also gives our neighbor some pleasure, the act is doubly charitable.

10 : "Cast Your Care Upon the Lord . . ."

ABOUT 2000 B.C. the Akkadians developed a rich civilization. Among the relics of their culture are many folk-proverbs as this one: "Whoever possesses much silver may be happy; whoever possesses much barley may be happy; but whoever has nothing at all can sleep." When a man owns too many things, he ends up being owned by them. The richest man in the world is the one who has all his desires gratified. Anyone, including a religious, who curtails his desires to the point that he needs no gratification, can be rich in this sense. Men of other religious persuasions of our own day, such as Albert Schweitzer and Mohandas Gandhi—whose deathbed possessions would not cover a small table top, teach religious men and women the importance of poverty. It is very pious to quote Christ's beatitude, "Blessed are the poor in *spirit*, for theirs is the kingdom of heaven," and justify extensive community, if not individual, possessions. But this is a subterfuge. The present chapter will consider both the common and the personal aspects of poverty, and whether up-dating justifies or encourages possession. Like every religious ideal in the history of mankind, once it becomes part of a stable institution, the implementation of poverty becomes mostly an individual effort.

Of every virtue Christ is the ideal. What did he say? "Do not take gold or silver or money in your belts, nor a knapsack for your journey, nor two tunics, sandals and staff, for the laborer deserves support." In this tenth chapter of St. Matthew, the reason Christ encourages laying aside encumbrances and not keeping extra supplies is that the people to whom he was sending the Apostles in that particular passage were the Jews. In verses five and six the Master commands them not to go to the towns of the Gentiles and Samaritans on their first missionary journey. Hence the importance of living from the people's donations, as the rabbis did then. How shall we understand Christ's words when he himself had a purse of money? Judas was the procurator of the twelve, as the Gospels point out. Then we know that Jesus had friends and disciples, who saw to his wants when he stayed in their town. St. Paul boasted that he sought no one's money, but supported his evangelical mission with the work of his own hands, for he was a tentmaker; therefore he, too, kept some reserve for his travels.

Scripture scholars are re-examining the Gospels and their meaning in the context of ancient life. With respect to the poverty of the Holy Family, some infer that Christ was not raised in utter poverty as the preachers like to affirm. He was born in a stable, it is true, but it was surely cleaner and more private than the caravanserai where St. Joseph first sought lodging. Bethlehem fulfilled the prophecy about David's ancestry of the Messiah, but the immediate reason for Joseph's registry in that town was possibly his ownership of some land in that area. In any case Galilee, where Christ passed most of his life,

was the best part of Palestine for a boy to grow up. The
better grazing land supported goats and sheep; the truck
gardens furnished fruits and vegetables in season. The
Sea of Galilee provided fish, and the vineyards produced
wine. The Holy Family surely had a garden of their own
around Nazareth, by which the income from St. Joseph's
carpentry was supplemented. Whereas the exile in some
ghetto of Egypt was difficult, I am sure, the boyhood and
early manhood of the Savior were probably secure
enough, although without luxuries. Otherwise we must
conclude that either Joseph was an incompetent artisan,
or God withheld his blessing from the three. Either conclusion is out of place.

When Christ began his public ministry there is no
doubt he lived in personal poverty, for he told an in-
quirer, "The foxes have holes and the birds of the air
have nests, but the Son of man has no place to lay his
head." But we must assume the Apostles and their leader
did not live in abject poverty, if Judas was a treasurer. In
the twenty-second chapter of St. Luke, verse thirty-six,
Christ directs the Apostles on the eve of his death to take
a purse and a knapsack and procure a sword. Perhaps the
Lord was suggesting their preparation for the missions to
the Gentiles, where they would not live from day-to-day
donations, as they had done in Palestine, but had to store
up provisions against the day of their world-wide disper-
sion.

Regardless how we view the life of Our Lord in these
exegetical problems, the broad sweep of his example
commits the religious attempting the Christ-life to poverty individually as well as collectively. Whereas individual poverty, both externally and internally, is a personal
matter, collective poverty must be interpreted according

to the apostolate of the order itself. Thus no one is excused from detachment and no one should accumulate what he or she cannot use as an individual. However, even in the strictest community one cannot *legislate* detachment and the law cannot cover every exigency and possibility of possession. Therefore houses of training must provide the example of older religious who live poorly, the actual environment of poverty, and the orientation of the young to attitudes of detachment, economy, careful use, and the importance of permissions.

It is not a fair conclusion that with the advent of the friars personal poverty began to be practiced individually for the first time in the history of religious orders. The Rule of St. Benedict did not grant many "possessions" besides his own clothes to a monk—a needle, work apron, tablets, and stylus. There was no place in the common dormitories—large rooms with rows of rush mats and blankets—to accumulate superfluities. Yet it is true that the monastery might be very wealthy. Of course, unlike small bands of friars in the towns, there was really no place for a hundred monks, for example, to beg their daily bread. Virtue has to be assessed, therefore, according to the environment in which it sprang up. Nevertheless, because laymen can neither see a violation of chastity or obedience, nor fully appreciate their onus, they tend to judge us as *religious* by our poverty even as they judge us as *apostles* by our charity.

This was one of the contributions of the mobile friars and later religious institutes—people could see individual and community poverty close at hand. As a community grows larger (this is the message of history), not only apostleship, initial zeal, and the service of love decline, but poverty is surrendered to the need of storing up provisions for a burgeoning institution. St. Bonaventure wrote in chapter sixteen of the *Rule for Novices* that voluntary poverty is the "first foundation of the whole spiritual edifice." Yet the foundation is rather obedience, to judge even by St. Francis, the spiritual father of St. Bonaventure. St. Francis submitted to the authority of the Church and Cardinal Hugolin when they amended his severity against those elements in the Franciscan Order which foresaw the accumulation of friaries and libraries to train incoming members. Finally, the great question, raised in the thirteenth century about poverty yet plagues religious orders today, but the plague is a beneficial kind of ulcer. It makes the individual judge whether he makes superfluity a necessity and luxury a habit, and it recalls the institute to its pristine virtue.

We are such creatures of environment who are quickly conditioned to needs of rest and relaxation, comfort and entertainment, diversion and finally luxury, that it takes a truck to move some male religious from one assignment to another. Women religious can rarely be criticized for serious violations of *external* poverty as individuals; in fact, they put men to shame. Among men, there are, however, many degrees and interpretations of poverty. What is permitted by the Constitutions determines where sin enters, nevertheless attachment and superfluity are reprehensible in all religious. Christ did not put any footnotes to his invitation, "Go, sell what you have, give it to the poor and you will have treasure in heaven; then come and follow me." There is a point beyond which rationalizations should not satisfy us and at which we ought to return to our novitiate concepts. Religious, whatever the apostolate, live by donations, mostly of people who enjoy less security than the religious. There is a corresponding obligation to use that money as befits a follower of Christ. There is no balm for any uneasy conscience to say the "extras" come from personal gifts or personal industry. We were not forced into religious profession, so every income is only by permission. I admit that the professional services of a priest, brother, or sister far exceed the compensation received by the order, nevertheless the individual cannot make that an excuse to live like other professional men with large incomes. These words are not a plea to throw out wristwatches, hobbies, vacations, all sports clothes and golf clubs. They are a warning that the danger to poverty is primarily in ourselves. The Scriptures call it the "lust of the eyes." A king who is content with one crown is poorer in spirit than a laborer who wants a second car he doesn't need.

How do we recognize individual poverty of both men and women religious? They have an indifference to the quality of their clothes and the furnishings of their room. They do not complain if their room is in an inaccessible or noisy part of the house, since the room must be occupied by someone. They put up with second-rate food and do not seek every opportunity to eat in restaurants or in the homes of benefactors. Their appliances and toilet articles are the essentials, not the sensual extras. They abhor accumulation of books they do not read, clothes they seldom wear, and especially money for which they have no permission. Their rooms do not look like religious-goods stores, especially of the avant-garde kind. They have a sense of value for tools, furniture, automobiles and house property, and use them economically not prodigally. They share their superfluities with others and periodically dispossess themselves of them. They do not consider shabbiness, dirt, or a slovenly desk the sign of detachment. They do not think themselves demeaned when they request permission to buy things, nor must they have the more expensive medicines, clothes and books. They do not seek benefactors to provide them with what the superior will not, often on the pretext of an apostolic need. Their hobbies, as permitted by the rules, are modest and really a relaxation, not a status symbol of which the affluent might be proud. They realize that the acid test of poverty is the spirit with which they would submit to the privation of anything given for their use or permitted by the superior and lawful custom. There is no point to draw out an elaborate examination of conscience. Violations of poverty are causes of strife in a household, even if only because of an exaggerated desire for equality. But if we understood, as the ancient saying went, that "a religious who owns a penny is not worth a penny," we would fear that we are making superfluity into commodity. Having been brought up in a nation of abundance, the religious tends to take abundance for granted. The time of training is endured and considered only a transitory state because the cost of running an institution admittedly prohibits even many conveniences. When we begin to "work for our keep," we assume that we acquire some title to abundance again. This double standard of poverty fosters the false notion that training is merely a temporary test of patience or an exercise in poverty which is merely academic, because the active life will be the door to all good things.

Of course I am not impressed by those religious on the opposite side of the street, who die and are found with a prayerbook and rosary as their sole personal possessions. It is a fortunate religious today who can be effective without certain *impedimenta* of their profession. Teach-

ers need visual aids and gadgets galore in their class-
rooms; preachers need scriptural commentaries, antholo-
gies and sermon series; administrators need references
and multigraphs and so on; brothers and home-makers
need trade magazines and expensive appliances. Every
country is different; every age has its own needs. Most of
these things are common property anyway. If a religious
has to borrow aspirins, a raincoat, a typewriter, he cannot
commend himself on his poverty. We are not living in
hard times, and many of these things are not luxuries
any more. By the same token, a hobby can be of great
benefit to the community: photography for recording
progress and special events, stamp-collecting to help the
missions, music to teach, art to decorate chapel appurte-
nances or the classroom, sports to attract vocations or
coach teams, and so forth. Of course a hobby's purpose is
relaxation rather than any kind of profit. Few religious
have blocks of free time to spend pursuing hobbies; those
who do will have to answer God for both the use of time
and possibly the excessive outlay of money from the community or—more likely—an interposed person.

The danger of violating poverty *collectively* exists for
both men and women. The superiors, as the leaders of
the community, must beware of assuming powers they do
not have by the law of the order and by the law of
Christ. For example, as I wrote in the chapter on obedience, expenditures depend on consent and counsel of the
higher superiors or the household. Even where this is not
verified, subjects would feel a more profound sense of
poverty and understand better the value of money if they
shared more in its spending. Similarly, superiors have no
right to alienate books or anything of appreciable value
and further use to the community, just because they are
in authority or wish to ingratiate themselves with outsid-

ers. What is common property is held by the superior in trust. Another source of disturbance to the consciences of subjects is the misappropriation of funds received by a member of the community for a specific purpose. A religious cannot receive a donation to which strings are attached until it is cleared with the authority. But if money is given the community for a specific purpose—whether for magazine subscriptions, a sacred vessel, or a poor family of the community's choice, no superior may accept the donation with the mental reservation of using it in any other way.

A larger problem of collective poverty is the number of religious institutions rising everywhere. They operate at tremendous cost and duplicate houses of training for a relatively small group of candidates. Many smaller communities must search their hearts to see if the erection of enormous structures is warranted. They are a scandal—in the radical meaning of a "stumbling block"—to laity and to the diocesan priests who feel the funds of the area are being drained needlessly. No one disputes the importance of separate novitiates and infirmaries. But those communities who have set up houses of study at Catholic colleges and universities have discovered not only is the cost less, with the community's teachers released for other assignments, but the education received is superior, because an isolated religious house cannot compete with the libraries, laboratory facilities and specialized teaching staff. A second benefit is the more realistic approach to future apostolates and an understanding of lay persons' problems by so many face-to-face contacts. The possibility of recruitment and the confirmation of one's own vocation is the result of a religious living the Christ-life within the flow of life's currents. Naturally these houses of study are not always feasible to larger communities.

Everyone likes a decent and convenient home, including religious. Accomodations for guests can be more elaborate. No one objects to money spent to beautify the house of God. But it is a mistake for religious to acquire mansions because they are donated, or when they are a drug on the market. Apart from high maintenance and repair costs, religious do not belong in mansions. It is doubtful that poverty is served in the long run. May that religious superior live a thousand years who refuses such benefactions kindly, or will not accept an acreage beyond what is necessary for the order's present use, forseeable expansion, and adequate privacy! These tax-free grants create ill-will within the faith and outside it.

In general, too many priests and religious are "chiselers," using their religious garb to wheedle discounts and bargains out of reluctant "benefactors." There is a false sense of "poverty of spirit" in those who pressure the unwilling with pietistic and naive phrases. Religious ought to make economical purchases, but not force their vow of poverty down another's throat. Of course when benefactors desire *freely* to aid us—whether from conviction or merely for tax write-offs—we have no right to refuse to benefit the community and give them a chance to win God's blessing.

St. Francis told his friars, "As the brothers turn away from poverty, so men will turn away from them. But if they cling to Lady Poverty, the world will support them, for they are given to the world for its salvation." And in the Rule the saint wrote, "They must be as pilgrims and strangers in this world, confidently seeking alms. This is that sublime height of exalted poverty that makes you, my dear brothers, heirs and kings of the kingdom of heaven, poor in earthly goods, but rich in virtue." When

St. Clare was ordered to live according to the Rule of St. Benedict, with added strictures about enclosures and the customs of San Damiano, poverty was of the most severe kind. When a succeeding Pontiff offered a relaxation by permitting fixed incomes and ownership of more land around a monastery, St. Clare refused. Finally, because of some sisters in other convents who desired to use the relaxations, St. Clare wrote an entirely new Rule, ratified two days before her death. In it she commanded the sisters to own neither house nor convent nor anything, but serve the Lord in poverty and humility.

The stress on even collective poverty dates from the period of the mendicants and associated women's orders. But it is impossible today to beg and simultaneously to carry on an apostolate; in many places it is likewise illegal and subject to punishment. Nevertheless the *privilege* of poverty remains alienable to our Christian witness today. If there is little detachment, much superfluity, and collective affluence not required by the apostolate of the religious order, it must be called by its proper name—a lack of faith and trust in God's merciful providence to see us through financial crisis. If we were dedicated men and women, without concern for financial matters beyond a reasonable supply of necessities, benefactors would support us adequately beyond what we earn ourselves. Cannot God see to our needs? This chapter's title reveals his divine policy: "Cast your care upon the Lord, and he will sustain you."

Let everything be in moderation, everything with mortification, nothing without permission. As we grow older in religious life, we gradually discover amid our abundance, that the only poverty is not to possess God.

11 : "Let Him Take It . . . "

WHOEVER coined the phrase, "as homely as sin," was singularly removed from reality. We cannot ignore the attraction of living dangerously, of seeking gratification from novelty, of the temporary triumph of sin. Some are virtuous merely from lack of opportunity of being vicious; others are virtuous merely because they prefer the more uneventful life of not risking entanglement with the courts and sanctions of society. Still others are virtuous merely because it is expected of them, not because they have no evil desire in their hearts. In none of these cases is the virtue supernatural. I venture to say it was not even natural goodness, but only a facade of conformity. Some ancient philosopher said virtue is its own reward—an equally naive statement. As long as vice is not carried to surfeit and abominable excess, sin is attractive. Otherwise teachers of ethics and preachers of morality would not be so hard put to convince sinners of the reward of virtue in its own right already upon earth. When we see the prosperity of unscrupulous businessmen, the popularity of Hollywood "sex-symbols," the apparent indulgence by the world of those who bounce from marriage to marriage, and the acceptance by society of alcoholic party-goers and prodigal spenders, we have a right to question a bald statement which makes virtue its own reward. Natural virtue is rewarded on this earth mostly when it is of such great proportions that other men applaud the wonder as they marvel at Grand Canyon.

What I have said of virtue in general is doubly true of purity, especially that of religious. They cannot claim virtue if they simply lack the opportunity of vice, if they entered religion before they understood what they were rejecting by the vow of chastity, or if they are merely inhibited by the society of their fellow-religious. Our Lord pointed out that a person of lustful thoughts has already committed adultery in his heart. Further, a religious who would experiment with sex, expose himself or herself to dangerous associations, or even indulge with complete abandonment *except for the fear of eternal damnation,* has never understood the full implication of the vow of chastity. This vow is not merely the rejection of marriage—although each of us must consciously at some time or another do exactly that. The vow of chastity includes the knowledge of the body's goodness, and the wholesome integrity of human love, and how it "fills out" the personality. But the religious sees further fulfillment, a greater expression of the body's goodness, and especially a higher integrity of the whole person in relation to an apostolate undertaken out of love of God.

But it is a sad mistake, as evidenced by religious and priests who defect and attempt marriage or its base counterfeits, to think of chastity as merely the means required to be free for apostleship. To live alone, sexually speaking, is the *consequence of living with God integrally.* Of course married people live with God, if they are in the state of grace. *The complement of either person in marriage is the other person, whereas the complement that integrates the personality of a religious is God himself.* Those clergymen who desire to change celibacy as the law of the Church, as well as those religious who lose God as their complement by laxity and weakened faith, have failed to realize this positive and far more important aspect of celibacy. I, plus a spouse, plus God, would for most of us be an unholy trinity, a triangle that would rival a daytime television series. What of Eastern Catholic clergymen who marry? If I read the statistics correctly most of them are monks, who do not marry. Also a bishop cannot have been married. Nor can a widowed priest re-marry—which seems a strange prohibition (found also in St. Paul), if the married state were so desirable for a man or woman of God *in itself*. And if I read the Fathers correctly, the married Apostles did *not* continue to live with their wives, once they accepted the call of Christ.

The vow of chastity, then, means finding the fulfillment of love, the satisfying complement of our personality, and the integrity of our body and our soul with God. Sex in all of its lawful and pleasurable expressions is a wonderful thing, but is set aside for a more wonderful relationship. I have never known a religious or priest who was faithful to meditation and contact with God in prayer daily, who wanted to return to the world of sex. But just as human love will not sustain itself without a sharing of emotional and intellectual—not just physical —intimacy, so our love of God will not sustain itself without the same intimacy. Like a crossed lover we bicker with God's demands—or place ourselves in the occasions of sin. Thus the supernatural virtue of chastity is not its own reward—a cheerless thought! God is its reward. As for our future life, the Scriptures speak of the virgins who follow the Lamb wherever he goes.

All the above paragraphs will not be entirely comprehended by younger and unformed religious. Without the *experience* of God's intimacy—"friendship" is too anemic a word—young religious know only of the struggle with purity, a terrible, seemingly endless corridor of darkness and depression. That is one reason why God gives them the saccharine delights of spiritual elation and consoling sweetness in prayer. We all know their impermanence. Those who train young religious must reinforce the thought that there is light at the end of the corridor—the enduring relationship of familiarity. Of course our arms ache to hold a lover, our bodies crave indulgence, our flesh trembles under the slightest pressure of another's touch: these are the good things for which nature has prepared all human beings. But this urgency is so constant that there is a need to teach young religious how to pray well, for this contact with their Lover is the only way to put some windows in the corridor. Although the wholesome friendships with our charitable co-religious and warm, human contacts with our families are supplementary to divine love, the latter alone will "complete" us as human beings. Some psychiatrists incorrectly maintain (if their statements are couched in the impoverished terms of nature without grace) that religious and priests are incomplete or immature without the ultimate expression of sex in marriage. They do not understand the higher substitution of God's personality for another human's personality. If they call it "only sublimation," we shall make the most of it!

Being children of a world which has more opportunities than ever before to disseminate sex knowledge and display sex through entertainment media, religious no doubt have the same enlarged interest and unsatisfied curiosity. Yet it is not enough for Christians characteristically to fall back on Platonic ideas that the soul is "enveloped and imprisoned" in the body. We think the body is only a poor country cousin of the soul. We refer to "the flesh" as "our enemy" with disdain. We tell the young that purity is the angelic virtue, and that we shall be like angels in heaven one day—which is a ridiculous notion. What a lop-sided universe such Christians dwell in! It is true that the operations of the soul, taken singly, are on a higher level, particularly because the soul is immortal and the body dies. But this last is so only because of original sin. After the general resurrection we shall return to our natural state forever as a composite of body and soul. Not only is the body a *handmaid* and necessary vehicle on earth, by which the soul learns and wills, it is also a *partner* that has different functions on earth, just as it will have a different glory in heaven—the agility of thought, immortality, the restored ability no longer to suffer and spiritualization that will permit its movement through solids as did Our Lord through the closed doors of the upper chamber. These are not insignificant qualities. Religious, even as all Christians, should keep this aspect of the body before them as an encouragement in matters of chastity.

The fact that a religious makes *instinctual* physical and emotional response to sex is exhausting to battle, but this human response does not make a man or woman unclean or depraved any more than hunger or sleepiness depraves us. It is *good* to be partly animal because God through the agency of nature *intends* us to be partly animal. We may die of old age without ever losing a strong sexual drive. If that is our destiny because of our physical constitution, humility indicates we accept ourselves as we are, patience demands that we laugh at our frailty, and chastity urges that we depend on old-fashioned remedies and mortifications. Another chapter is dedicated to bodily discipline and emotional maturity; the virtues are all interrelated. To judge from the writings by and about even the saints, temptations are unavoidable. Everything that we see, hear, smell, touch and taste makes its impression on our bodily senses—and through them upon the soul —according to the meanings and viewpoints and interests to which we are conditioned for many years before entering religious life.

After a person reaches puberty, one of the interests irrevocably attached, for example, to a television drama about even pure human love is a sexual one. The practice of dismissing or discounting this meaning in any sense-impression received is itself a conditioned process. Married persons need not discount this interest, as long as it is not sinfully manifested and fulfilled outside of marriage. Because religious cannot so express themselves without sin, either they successfully condition their responses to temptation, or they absent themselves from the sources of sin. If neither is possible, they had best leave the religious life; this is a fact, however, to be ascertained during the probation period, not delayed for several years. However, I believe many young religious would not leave the houses of training prematurely, if they were properly counseled on *conditioning,* on temptation, on the importance of gradual self-conquest through contact with God by prayer.

When the religious who has been professed for some

years, as well as the priest who has been ordained a while, experiences sudden doubts of chastity or the recurrence of weakness, two things must be clearly understood. First, he or she is irrevocably committed to God, and defection is no solution, for "the last state becomes worse than the first," without the helps of religion, yet with all the burdens of chastity and sin remaining. Second, if the religious, prior to the "attack," has been successful in living up to the obligations of chastity, it is a clear mandate that he or she must return to those practices that made earlier success possible. As I said of apostolic zeal, of the service of love called obedience, and of poverty, so chastity needs the same implementation throughout our whole religious life. "Let him who is strong take heed lest he fall." We need a constant response to our vocation on every level. Older religious can no longer quote, "Let him take it who can," but rather, "No one who puts his hand to the plow and looks back is fit for the kingdom of God."

Many "authorities" among religious in recent years have decried the existence of preparatory seminaries and postulancies as depriving the young of the typical experience, including dating, of teenagers. Once more, the time to enter religion is when God calls. If conditioning to the sexual meanings of all our sense-perceptions is important, then the training of young religious has the importance of preparing them for their vow of chastity and initiating them into that all-important prayer-life that will support it. There is no reticence about sex in the ordinary high school, hence God may have a divine purpose in calling the young so early, including those who ultimately leave. The young should not be left in a vacuum excluding all sex knowledge. Even as such knowledge is imparted according to the proportionate need of their age, the positive values of chastity can be taught. Fewer religious would have problems of chastity if the unfit were weeded out earlier and the fit trained prudently to overcome habits and attitudes of sin. The period of training in chastity is never over, even for seasoned religious. The Legion of Decency ratings are for them, too. Some television shows, particularly the suggestive raconteurs late at night, are inappropriate. Magazines and novels deserve careful selection. The importance of sincere and forthright confessions cannot be over-estimated—no hedging, no glosses, no justifications. Double-meaning stories—or worse, sad to say—are the signs of weakened faith in one's vocation and the loss of intimacy with God. Yet there is also the comforting thought of St. Augustine, no stranger to the profligate life himself: "A long-lived chastity is held [by God] as virginity." Let it never be said of the mature sister, priest or brother who taught purity by word and external example, at least, that "others he saved, himself he cannot save." This taunt offered to Christ on the cross by the Sanhedrin will surely be given by the devils to foolish religious in hell.

Religious with weakness or perversion in matters of sex cannot expect to find a solution in mere stop-gap procedures as a transfer, a change of assignment, medicines and pills, natural psychotherapy, or anything else on a purely natural level. If there *is* any danger in the young entering religion too early, it is the danger that the inhibitions of the cloister and life of vows—obvious and necessary inhibitions—prevent outspoken declaration of needs and the natural flowering of their personality and the warm, human inter-personal relationships with others, if the training is inadequate. That is why the current emphasis on active apostolates even by seminarians and aspirants is so timely and so badly needed. Sex problems, including those of religious, are rooted in nature, and one cannot ignore natural solutions. But since these problems are contingent upon sin and spiritual guilt, the rehabilitation of a stricken soul must be a *total re-alignment* of all his or her attitudes to the order of grace. Such a person must accept God anew to replace a sinful liaison. Readjustment of personality does not mean that sinful attraction, even a perversion, will automatically disappear, any more than anyone's temptations will disappear suddenly without prolonged conditioning. The humility to accept oneself and admit the need for help is the beginning that is required. I do not believe any religious or priest with deep-seated problems of chastity can be aided as well by any other specialist, as by a *priest-confessor trained in psychology.* So many excesses in sex are traceable to anger over and dissatisfaction with one's own lack of holiness or professional competence, that the counselor must himself understand religious life.

As in all of the virtues religious are called upon to manifest, their chastity is the most sublime expression of a human-divine relationship. A religious stands in the current of contemporary life to illustrate that chastity is not only possible, but desirable. Because chastity, normally speaking, is possible only by grace, a religious does not despise the world when it fails in chastity, but understands its need for an example of the Christ-life. Not only to those outside the faith, but to those of our own religious convictions, the religious shows purity is possible in marriage, and self-restraint is possible outside of marriage.

12 : Puritanism
in Religious Life

THE NATURAL SEQUEL to a chapter on purity is a discussion of its counterfeit, puritanism. It has been the bane of the religiously minded throughout the history of Christendom. Actually, in its theological implications, it is almost the worship of evil, or at least that is its historical origin. In the childhood of the human race, when monotheism was all but lost to mankind—except for that strain running through human history which flowered into Judaism—even sophisticated cultures worshiped principles of evil. The Graeco-Roman theogony, and others as well, gave human qualities to the principles of good and evil that seemed to run the world. That is why the Fathers of the Church referred to the pagan gods as devils —as anthropomorphisms of the "prince of this world," as Christ himself called Satan.

It yet seems to primitive peoples today that evil prevails over good when they see sickness, pain, death, poverty, hunger. Hence their shamans look to propitiate the demons of evil, rather than seek the favor of the good deities. They do not placate demons as the opponents of Christ, of course, but only as the powers of darkness. But the Christian philosopher does not teach that evil is "embodied," that is, that there are powerful, supernatural beings which are fundamentally or essentially evil. Even the devil is good in so far as he is a creature sustained in existence by the divine power he sought to equal. If nothing created is evil, what is the source of sin and accidents and disease?

The problem of evil has been the subject of philosophy, drama and poetry since mankind became literate. The Christian solves it by pointing out that the disordered universe is the result of the original sin of Adam. Whatever evils, as war and disease, are contingent on the human will at least originally stem from the perversity of the weakened intellect and will of the sons of Adam. This is the evaluation of the moralist. The metaphysician in turn says that evil cannot exist as an independent being —like the pagan principle of evil—but only within a good being as the *lack* of what *should* be there.

What has this to do with puritanism and the religious life? As God finished each "day's" work of creation, the writer records the Lord as "seeing it was good." The moral and metaphysical truth taught in Genesis is that all creation is good until perverted by man's free will in the unlawful use of what is basically good. The very multiplication of man through childbirth was reckoned evil by the medieval Albigensian heresy; one "committed" marriage. The "perfect" state—which a person delayed in entering until at the brink of death—did not permit even eating, because all matter was evil in itself. St. Augustine toyed with similar concepts before his conversion—under the label of Manichaeism, which provided that its adherents live by dietary laws that would save them from excessive "materialism."

Puritanism, or American Calvinism, as a religion is practically defunct in the United States, but its spirit survives in "blue laws," which forbid, for example, the sale of liquor or parties on the Sabbath and in some localities at any time. Yet alcohol is not evil in itself. The prudish Victorian age, as another example, wished to impose sanctions on the subject of sex to the point of not placing books by male authors next to books by female authors on the same shelf! The philosophical error of such practices, which were entirely external and did not prevent unseen sin, much less the attitude of sin, was that pleasure is a "necessary evil," but one about which decent people didn't talk. The pseudo-Catholic version of Puritanism is Jansenism, whose heretical tenets sound so devout and plausible that they still linger on in Catholic thought. Jansenism seems to teach that only a few Catholics make it to heaven. The righteous ought to fear God's stern justice. No one ought approach him in Holy Communion unless right after confession without even the trace of a venial sin. Thus the Eucharist is a reward for the good, instead of the remedy of sin and support of the weak, according to the mind of the Master, who said he came to save sinners, because the healthy have no need of a physician.

The remnants of Jansenism are mirrored in religious lives. Certainly not in the worship of evil, but in the dour attitude that makes "the world" a hotbed of only wickedness; in the unbalanced attitude that makes offenses against the sixth commandment the worst; the joyless attitude that makes pleasure, spontaneous humanity and laughter the warning signs of laxity. This concept often makes religious erroneously consider the sacrament of matrimony inferior to the religious state. After all, religious do not exist in Church life to point out to others what they *might* have become, if it only weren't for their weaknesses and disabilities. The moralists of the Middle Ages—all priests or religious—urged lay persons not to exercise their marriage rights before Holy Communion and all during Lent, a custom that still obtains in the Eastern Church. Whereas this is heroic virtue and hence commendable if done freely, the acts of marriage are themselves virtuous acts of love and hence meritorious. The negative attitude is reinforced by certain misunderstood passages of Sacred Scripture, as the psalm verse, "In sins did my mother conceive me."

Some handbooks of spirituality for novices call the fondling of a child and stroking of a fur-bearing animal types of sensuality—not sin, but apparently dangerous indulgence. Christ with the children, and St. Francis with the birds and the wolf of Gubbio might have received stern warnings from their superiors. The morose and unapproachable religious may have learned that his state in life is a joyous one to be consummated in the eternal bliss of heaven, but he has no external appearance of being destined for heaven. True sanctity never exists without austerity—at least interior mortification in the lives of those incapable of corporal mortification—but austerity is not co-terminous with holiness. Pagan philosophers, athletes in training, dieters because of vanity or health and others practice austerity totally unrelated to the order of grace. Two chapters will explore the value and necessity of mortification.

One of the loveliest and spiritually most accurate examples of the place of sensual gratification in our lives is described in a magazine article about a group of Carmelite cloistered nuns. Of course they voluntarily cut themselves off from many legitimate pleasures of life in order to seek God. Some years ago this convent was allowed to have a radio overnight, in order to listen to the canonization of St. Pius X. They also received permission to listen to a symphony orchestra under Sir Malcolm Sargent. Some of the nuns had not heard any music for as long as thirty years and were so awestruck by the exquisite musical phrases suddenly coloring their lives, that they wrote a letter of thanks to the conductor. "We were left just praising God in giving such gifts to man. We cannot show our gratitude by applause nor by coming to another concert, but we have our job to do for God and we include you and all the orchestra in that. . . . One day we hope that the loveliness of the things of God that we are occupied with will fall on your ears as strikingly and compellingly as your music came to us."

These sisters understood that the beauty of nature and the outpourings of man's mind are foretastes of heaven and samples of divine beauty and intelligence. They also gave witness to the purposeful austerity of their lives and the true value of sensual gratification as a stepping-stone to heaven. Their Christ-life also gave a new dimension to the world of those musicians.

St. Bonaventure wrote a treatise, *De Reductione Omnium Artium ad Theologiam,* which might loosely be translated, "How All Branches of Knowledge Are Subdivisions of Theology." In the tradition of his order, the Seraphic Doctor looked upon the universe as a detective seeking clues; he saw all about him the traces, *vestigia,* which is better translated as the "footprints" of God. Someone once wrote that we ought to wander through creation as a little boy tiptoes through a museum, or better, through a candy factory! Religious should find even more evidence of the providence of God towards man and his creativity in nature with simple awe, not because they are naively pietistic, but because to them most of all these wonders should proclaim, "We *are* lovely and yet we fade and perish, but you take care, for you go on forever!"

Franciscan theologians have had a kind of holy fixation on the basic goodness of all men and on the holiness of the created world as a "sign" of the Creator. They teach that God in fact so loved human nature as the crown of visible creation, as the link between the worlds of matter and spirit, and as the summation of the mineral, vegetable, animal and intellectual universe, that he would have sent his Son upon earth whether Adam sinned or not. This is not a hypothetical question of whether the Word would have become incarnate man if Adam had remained loyal. The Franciscans teach that God was so enamoured of his human creature and so expectant of the glory he would receive from man, that his divine mission of the Son was God's eternal decree, as the angels' song on the first Christmas suggests: "Glory to God in the highest," and secondly, because of Adam's sin, "peace on earth to men of good will."

Just as all paternity on earth is structured on the fathership of God in heaven, says St. Paul, so, analogously, our humanity is structured after a pattern of Jesus Christ. Since the first objective willed by a person is the last to be accomplished—as the house is completed only after the preliminary structures of foundation, walls and roof —so Christ came only in the fullness of time. He came primarily to be a loving and beloved example to us, and only secondarily for our salvation, as the Nicene Creed indicates by the phrase, "Who for us men and for our salvation descended from heaven." Thus God's special glory, received from the incarnate Son, who is to be the exemplar of our service to God and to each other, is the primary "motive" of the Incarnation. The effect of this teaching should be a joy in creation as the mirror of God, a feeling of our intrinsic value in God's eyes, a greater awareness of our dignity and responsibility as the crown of a godly universe, and an even "natural" brotherhood with Christ.

This is the very antithesis of the puritanical spirit in religious life. In her "little way" of spiritual formation, the Little Flower considered even the meager joys allowed to her community—a feastday meal, a little warmth from the stove—as foretastes of heaven. I stress that her gratifications were meager, lest anyone make her attitude a license to overindulge in even the lawful pleasures of religious, which are the more satisfying because of their rarity. I remember a religious who would say a "much obliged!" to the Lord, when he saw a particularly beautiful landscape or deer by the road as he drove along. When he saw the city skyscrapers, read about the achievements of astronauts or pushed a button that saved him time and effort, he would say a "much obliged!" to the Lord, because he saw the world is good. Such a religious, who does not shrink from human fellowship and the good uses of the world, is not only more awake to its needs, but also more grateful to God for the personal blessings of skillful hands, a well-proportioned body, an alert mind, an amiable personality, an education, loyal friends, and so forth, because they are helps in the apostolate.

A special point to be made in the context of "puritanism" is the importance of teaching others proper attitudes about sex. Our religious state, which manifests the self-discipline the world admires, is an actual help in teaching sex matters. (Priests, of course, are trained to teach the morality of the sixth and ninth commandments and to impart contingent sex facts in the counseling room and confessional. Sisters and brothers who lack this specific training in moral theology may do untold harm in group and individual guidance.) Here I have reference to the "facts of life"; every educator and counselor must be ready to speak matter-of-factly and informally to those who ask or need this information according to their age and whose parents have failed to communicate it. Yet a teacher, counselor, hospital attendant or social worker who must touch on these sensitive matters would fail his religious calling unless he reinforced the positive values of sex control by teaching as well at least some basic principles of moral guidance. Young and old alike want clear concepts of mortal and venial sins, and there is no reason why sisters should not explain this to girls and male religious to boys. The inability to do so gracefully, almost casually, indicates a hiatus in their training as religious or some emotional gaps in their own spiritual lives. Of course, no one is graceful and casual as a beginner. Nor should the priest, brother or sister feel inhibited by the smirks and grins of adolescents, who may just be hiding their embarrassment. Apart from this possibility, we must remember that many aspects of sex are touched by humor, such as the awkwardness of the young in dating and their confusion upon entering the adult world.

To avoid the pitfall of puritanism, religious teachers, particularly priests in the pulpit, should refer to the dignity of the human person in the light of the primary motive of the Incarnation, as was outlined earlier in this chapter, and the error of Jansenism in keeping people from Holy Communion, which the Council of Trent declared a help in overcoming the concupiscence of the flesh. They should stress that God designed the *entire* body and gave it the capacity to express holy love in marriage, not self-gratification. Knowledge of sex is essential to mature persons, but knowledge of itself does not lead to virtue or self-control; in fact, given in overdoses, it can throw both the sins and virtues related to sex out of proportion. Most confessors, counselors and teachers tend to err by omission. Pubertal changes, personal hygiene, and the "why" of marriage can be noted in proper course, but not to mixed groups. It is a strange policy of some schools to leave the teaching of sex-related knowledge to the clinical atmosphere of the biology course, but to shy away from a frank discussion in religion classes, where the morality and spiritual resources can better be handled. I feel this is such an important topic that the techniques and limits of sex instruction and morality should be part of the training or renewal programs of religious and priests.

Occasionally there will be excesses, as the grade-school teacher who had her children read aloud in class portions of a novel about teenagers. Although the book had lewd and vulgar words, the sister considered the "literary" experience justifiable, because "the youngsters probably talked that way on the playground"! The pendulum swings to the other side in the case of the nuns who are instructed that it is immodest to fail to wear the armlet or sleevelet. It may be disobedience or even contempt, if it is done maliciously, but scarcely immodesty. Incredible though it sounds, a priest who aided a foundress in drawing up the customs and rules of her new community, advised the mother that it was a mortal sin to scratch an itch on the arm under the sleevelet! Whereas this ridiculous moral concept did not become a part of the community's tradition, some of the attitudes engendered plague the spiritual development of individual nuns yet today.

13 : The Mortification
of Atonement

MORTIFICATION, however you look at it, is supposed to be painful. The purpose of mortification is more than to discipline the body and mind into a more willing service by denying them even some of the innocuous pleasures of life. Its purpose is also to live a fuller Christ-life by imitation, in smaller doses, of the privations and passion of Christ. Christ did not have to curb himself, because his passions were orderly, his emotions were directed into proper channels, and his body and soul were committed fully to the service of the apostolate. Yet he did live a life of mental and physical agonies because of our human need of example. Christ foresaw the martyrdoms and guillotine and concentration camps and, as teacher, wanted to show that the Master did as much as any disciple, and the disciple is not above the Master if he does suffer. So Christ tells his potential followers in St. Matthew's Gospel to deny themselves, take up their cross daily and follow him.

Equally important from the psychological viewpoint is that mortification, so galling to our desire for well-being, makes it plain to us how far we have yet to go in quieting our more outrageous demands. If we can barely stand a headache without snapping at others, complaining to our companions, and multiplying medications, it should be clear that something is lacking in our self-mastery. Shakespeare wrote that there was never a philosopher who could endure a toothache patiently. Of course, as a few saints observed, after years of the reluctance of their mind and body to come to heel, mortification became so much a way of life, they wondered if it was even meritorious any more. This will always remain a speculative question for most of us. However, I want to add at once that, merit or not, there is no record that the saints gave up their practices of self-discipline.

The most naive concept of mortification is either that God enjoys it, or that you're supposed to—at least at some time in the dim future. Nothing could be farther from the truth. God expects us to use our brains to destroy sickness, poverty, privation and pain. God is not a sadistic Being, gloating over human misfortune. A religious or lay person has a sad notion of his God, moreover, if he thinks that the bearing of suffering is a kind of contract with God: so much pain for so many favors. This notion is on a par with the persons who make novenas, pilgrimages and other worthwhile religious exercises without true resignation in prayer. They try to bargain with God, using suffering for collateral. No! God is not pleased by suffering, which is a consequence of original sin anyway, but only by the *motive* with which we bear our problems and pains: the imitation of Christ, the fuller subjection of self to the apostolate, the example to others that human suffering has value. Any other idea of God is a perversion in religion.

The other side of the coin is that we are supposed to

enjoy mortification itself; this, too, is a psychologically warped notion. The fact is that we are to bear a problem *despite* our dislike. There is no perversion, however, in feeling proud of self-mastery and even in taking joy in a disciplined body, a mortified curiosity, or a tractable will. But we should not look upon ourselves as *possessing* a body, mind, imagination, emotion, or will power (although we speak that way) which are to be manipulated by us as by an independent computer. We *are* our faculties in operation, our decisions, our laughter, our daydreams. When we are in the "purgative" or initially very active level of spiritual life, we tend to isolate our faculties and try to mortify them according to the spiritual writers' suggestions, individually and one by one. Thus a young religious may decide never to use a handrail going upstairs or a soft chair (in order to harden his body); he may consciously refuse to look out a window or delay to read a letter from loved ones a few days, in order to kill his curiosity; he may deliberately eat the food he dislikes in order to mortify his palate; he may plan to recreate with a companion he despises in order to thwart his emotions. These are fruitful exercises. If they appeal and are helpful, they should be continued. Those who consider them maudlin, useless or pedantic, probably need them most of all.

As the religious matures, however, this compartmented mortification is absorbed into a more generalized attitude of self-control. Our increasing intimacy with Christ and easy, familiar conversation with him helps us to become more disciplined in the sense we give our energies and self-scrutiny directly to the positive actions of our apostolate. Instead of continually turning our minds upon ourselves and counting petty victories over sense—

frequently a source of pride, the personality of Christ engulfs us as a mantle. The earlier type of mortification is merely "putting off the old man"; it is actually useless unless we "put on the new man." An analogous example is telling a tempted person to scourge his body, starve his stomach, tire out his body and sleep on the floor. This is not bad advice; it is often helpful. Better counsel might be to advise "putting on the new man," recognizing the presence of God in his body, reflecting on the crucifixion, seeing God as the complement of his love-relationship, and looking to the glorious resurrection of his body.

Have I played down the old-fashioned mortifications? No—we shall always need some self-inflicted coercions. But motivation is not to be a "contract" with God. Yet the saints appear to have multiplied their penances. (I am not referring to the staggering corporal discipline which some saints practiced by a divine inspiration after they were so well-formed, so that pride could gain no foothold as a result of their heroism.) Let me approach the "problem" of mortification in saints' lives in the following way. There is no doubt that *atonement* for even lesser sins is a quality of love. But atonement also must come from right inner need: not of reprisal against self, nor as the sudden result of disgust after a fall into sin, but as a means of repaying divine justice and restoring the balance of order in the soul. Therefore the most appropriate atonement is to practice the positive acts of the virtue which was upset by our vice. This is not, as some would have it, a guilt complex seeking forgiveness by hostility to self; it is true and actual guilt, seeking to restore balance in the choices of our will after God has forgiven us. Sin is in the will; vice is a series of wrong choices; the will regains its Christ-like equilibrium by positive acts that compensate for specific sins. Thus the uncharitable person must, in his atonement, seek the occasion to be generous, to be tolerant, to be forgiving. He must especially seek out the person offended and confront him with plain-spoken understanding and love. To live side by side in a kind of mutual agreement to avoid confrontation and exchange is not atonement, not charity, and especially not mortification. As in every virtue, so with mortification: an apostolic effectiveness coincides with personal sanctification. Instead of keeping a tiresome mental record of when and if we have performed something irritating to our senses or faculties—rather like picking off snipers in guerilla warfare—it is better to put on Christ and exercise ourselves in the positive acts of virtue opposed to our vices. After all, the purpose of all asceticism is mysticism—that is, the reason behind bodily and mental calisthenics is to run better in the race to God. Some saints, all of whom are guides in the race, seem to have stressed a certain kind of mortification, as St. Francis de Sales' control of temper by sweetness of disposition to the irksome; and St. John Berchmans' devotion to community life by his ready availability to his bothersome companions; and St. Margaret of Cortona's hairshirts and chains. Although each saint is surely mortified and self-controlled in all senses and faculties, were not these emphases actually acts of atonement for sin, at least venial sin? At least the biographies of these saints reinforce this hypothesis.

Someone pointed out once that the capacity to suffer voluntarily is a distinctly human privilege denied to angels and the blessed. This is not meant to be a sop to us; suffering is still difficult. It is another way of saying that the angels and saints cannot intensify their Christ-life (if angels can even be properly included in Christ-life), because angels do not and saints no longer have passions capable of greater spiritual formation. As the macrocosm of universal creation is good, so the microcosm of our soul's passions is good. Unfortunately our language identifies passion with vice, whereas each of the seven passions is a drive that is necessary to human survival and well-being. *Intemperance* in food or drink is the excess of the good craving to eat well for our health, just as *sloth* is the excess of the drive that makes us seek sleep and relaxation. *Lust* is the misdirected sex urge that both expresses human love and keeps the human race going. *Avarice* is the need to own property for security and the care of dependents, but carried too far. *Pride* in our human dignity, our vocation, our share in the divine life through grace, our desire to achieve and be successful as teachers, preachers, mechanics or ditch-diggers is the proper mental attitude; the absence of pride in these areas is reprehensible. Similarly we should be *envious* of those who outstrip us in sanctity or professional ability, if it is because of our negligence. *Anger* is the extreme form of rightly-oriented indignation against war, poverty, crime and whatever degrades the individual and society; without it, there would be too little drive and enthusiasm in our apostolate.

Once more, when a basically good drive is thrown out of order by sin, the mortification needed is acts of the opposed virtues which restore balance in the soul and body. The *proud* religious does well to seek out or not avoid opinionated persons, who will challenge his views. He will quietly submit in his younger days to the censorship of his mail. The *avaricious* religious gets rid of superfluous possessions and does not complain if he is given a second-hand habit or piece of luggage. He does not acquire hobbies, sports clothes or an expensive wrist-watch merely as status symbols. The religious prone to *lust* accepts the lack of heat in the house or church during winter and the humidity of summer months with all the aches and pains of his body. The religious *envious* of others' degrees, family position, influence with the superior or preaching ability, does not criticize, but admits his inferiority without petulance against God for not creating him with greater abilities. He does not even envy those who have facility in prayer, but submits to dryness in cold faith. The *intemperate* religious reduces his intake of food and drink, and avoids alcohol and tobacco altogether, if he feels a compelling urge for them. Whereas moderate alcohol and tobacco are not sinful and may be useful for relaxation, if the craving is very strong, it is better for a religious to give it up entirely rather than cut down, which is difficult for most of us. For example, if a priest curtails his thanksgiving after Mass to have a smoke, I don't say he is sinning, but I do say his attachment prevents growth in holiness. The religious inclined to *anger* counteracts this urge by seeking out bores for company, at least occasionally, and by submitting to the ribbing that may needle him. He maintains the silence, endures the incompetence of others and applies himself to distasteful tasks particularly when he feels frustrated. The *slothful* religious forces himself to the monotonous and unrewarding tasks early in the day; he is wary of prolonged siestas not needed to keep him alert and wakeful during the rest of the day.

Not all of these mortifications are typical of one religious. For example, I don't know of any sisters who smoke. Many male religious, especially in parochial life, cannot keep the grand silence in a busy household. The mail of priest-religious is not subject to censorship, because they receive confidential information. Sisters do not wear sports clothes, unless up-dating progresses uncommonly fast. What must be sought is the attitude that seeks *mortification of the particular passions and predominant faults.* Even male religious, who tend to be amused by sisters' submission to mortification and simple acceptance of religious principles of asceticism, may remember that when they were novices, they, too, thought that such conscious self-discipline was important, and to judge by their subsequent state of soul, their indulgence in alcohol or gambling, and their ineffectual or non-existent prayer-lives, they would be glad on their death-beds to exchange their spiritual status for that of an "amusing" novice, simple nun or obscure brother of the community. As I said, to "put on Christ" is our aim, but I do not know of any religious who did, until he "put off the old man." It is the devil who is having the last laugh on these religious sophisticates who smile at medieval, old-fashioned piety. The simple idealism of young religious should be like that of the high-school football players, who submit to the deliberate berating of their coach and the prohibition of soft drinks, tobacco and late hours for a transitory achievement. The youngsters even tolerate the coach's demand for a crew haircut, even though a hair style does not seem directly to improve their tackling and passing. Yet older religious lightly set aside the lessons of the novitiate designed to make them athletes of Christ and often look upon these practices as "kid stuff."

Although the danger is that we make too little atonement rather than too much, I wish to add a footnote to the paragraphs above for the sake of religious, particularly the younger, who might be discouraged at facing an endless series of mortifications. Father Augustine Baker in his book, *Holy Wisdom,* which apparently has been too long out of print for such a masterpiece, cites the dangers of some authors' advice to religious. In matters which are indifferent (without goodness or evil in themselves) we ought not to seek always what is the most contrary to our natural inclinations, as eating the least-liked food or seeking the most tiresome co-religious. We should not live in "continual contradiction and crossing of nature." Particularly in immature religious—a quality that has nothing to do with age—these self-inflicted mortifications nourish self-esteem as well as contempt for others not so courageous. It is folly and inexcusable pride for those, who with a shallow prayer-life scarcely bear the mortifications imposed by community life, still attempt others devised by themselves. Further we may stifle our own liberty by multiplied obligations. It is probably of little help against our sloth in prayer, for example, to add many vocal prayers, because it may prejudice our existing vocal prayers of obligation and leave too little time for peaceful thought and recollection. It is more wholesome to strive against spiritual sloth and melancholy by the direct contact of contemplative prayer, rather than by using the vocal prayers someone else wrote.

Further, any mortification, such as depriving ourselves of enough sleep so that we are not alert in our assigned tasks the next day, especially mental tasks, is in vain. Our ensuing irritability and sluggishness make us unfit. The saints had years of ascetical preparation before they attempted this, and it may well have been the exception, rather than the rule, that they passed whole nights in prayer. Conversely, I would rather see religious participate without haste in the liturgy inside an air-conditioned Chapel, than observe them rushing through with great hurry to escape the airless confines of a chapel that probably inhibits (not prevents) the true prayer of contact with God. I would praise the mortified religious who gives up colognes, but not the one who stops using dandruff-remover!

I often advise devout lay persons who attend daily Mass, but complain of dryness and mechanical reception of Holy Communion, to come to church only five or six days a week. It is wise not to thwart nature endlessly. It is helpful to "reward" ourselves occasionally, especially in times of depression, with entertainments and relaxations from the daily round of rules and prohibitions. Not a few religious just need more sleep and plenty of nourishing food to help cure melancholy and frustrations. I have heard of the prudent superiors of nuns, who are allowed to attend any of the parish Sunday and holyday Masses at their leisure, say their own morning prayers privately, and cook their own breakfast when they choose, in order to shake themselves free of the bonds of unremitting routine and renew their spirit for the coming week.

Particularly, young religious should seek advice and "permission" from their confessor or some director before adding spiritual exercises and mortifications of their own choosing. Not only is there the added light from another's opinion added to the spirit of obedience, but the fact we have revealed our intention to someone else tends to spur us forward when our spirit slackens.

Finally, St. Francis warned his friars who had chosen the ascetical way of life, "Let them not judge those whom they see dressed in soft and fine clothes and who partake of dainty food. Let each person rather judge and despise himself."

14 : The Mortification
of the Moment

AT THE TIME when Eastern monasticism flourished, the monasteries were located in the deserts and atop mountains. To protect themselves from marauders the monks either built a high wall around the monastery or built it on inaccessible crags where scaling ladders were useless. In fact, in some places incoming supplies and outgoing monks had to be raised and lowered in a huge basket on pulleys—the antecendents of our elevators. St. Pachomius, that ever-present figure in the *Lives of the Fathers,* presided over such a sequestered monastery. Among his subjects was a young and eager monk, who longed for martyrdom.

St. Pachomius instructed him to obey the existing rules and endure the regular mortifications. But it was not enough for the young man. As soon as he heard that the Saracens were terrorizing the area, he simply had to try to convert them; actually he was nursing the hope of a glorious martyrdom. St. Pachomius reluctantly agreed to his importuning. No sooner than out of the monastery, the young monk set about his task. However, the Saracens apparently had some missionary spirit, too, and tried to force him to adore their god. He boldly refused to worship an idol at first. But a little torture, skillfully applied, destroyed his resistance. Finally, after beating him and deriding his foolish pride, the Saracens left the young monk at the foot of the monastery, more dead than alive.

The moral of the story is that no one is ready for a heroic death until he is leading a heroic life, that is, the unsought mortification of the present moment, laid upon us by our state in life, is a daily martyrdom. The radical meaning of the word, "mortification," is "causing death." The acceptance of daily frustrations, problems, pains, heartaches, and weaknesses of our bodily functions is better for most of us than ten years of self-imposed mortifications. The subject of the previous chapter was self-imposed mortification; a book about the religious life cannot ignore the importance of such ascetical practices. I advised religious to restrict themselves to the mortification of *atonement*. This chapter is about the mortification of the *passing moment* imposed upon us by the providence of God and our religious state.

Every Rule and Constitutions of a religious order approved by the Holy See is a guaranteed method of achieving sanctity and saving our soul. When the Holy Father, directly or through the Sacred Congregations, speaks on a matter as important as a religious family's Rule and apostolate, it is an expression of the ordinary *magisterium,* or teaching authority of the Pope. It is not itself an infallible pronouncement, but when the community bears the fruit of holy members and even canonized saints, who lived according to that rule, a faithful member has the most concrete evidence of the certainty of salvation. Hence the mortifications of our state in life pursuant to the Rule and Constitutions—were they but observed without subterfuge—would themselves be sufficient for salvation without the multiplication of self-imposed "suffering." Once more, since love seeks atonement, it appears that religious who observe their profession rather perfectly also add the mortifications of atonement. The Rule of a congregation represents the *common* means to a goal, just as the liturgy is the common expression of Christian worship. But as the liturgy is a *springboard* for private prayer, so the Rule is the *beginning* of additional spiritual exercises of choice. I venture to say that the liturgy of Mass, Divine Office, Benediction, and other liturgical worship proper to a community, such as investiture and profession, if they were *prayed* through reflectively and meaningfully, would guarantee a spirit of recollection all day without additional vocal prayers. The parallel is with the Rule. If it were truly observed without gloss, and if each superior and house provided the adequate environment and customs to make that observance possible, I venture to say additions of self-discipline would be superfluous even for those anxious to make great speed in spiritual growth. For this reason a spiritual director should be quite reluctant to urge these additional prayers and mortifications upon anyone who has not kept the *common* rules *uncommonly* well.

A case in point that ought to be also a comfort for the religious who has begun poorly in religious life is St. Hyacintha Mariscotti. She was a wild and capricious young woman, so that she was rejected by potential suitors again and again. She finally was so bored with her wealthy and purposeless life, that she decided to be a Tertiary Franciscan Sister. Yet she still did not make much of a break with her past; her religious life was just another novelty. Seventeenth-century canon law was not always specific, and the strictness of some convents was a matter of local option. It was also quite common for a woman, especially an older woman or a widow, to bring a sizeable dowry, take a room in a cloister and become a part-time religious, in so far as she had freedom to come and go, to receive visitors and to observe common life at her discretion.

Hyacintha took the broadest view of her religious state. She took a suite of rooms, had a maid and cook to prepare something more palatable than convent fare. Her habit was made of expensive cloth. She received visitors and gossiped with the experience of practice. While not excusing the laxity and at least the venial sins, particularly of scandal, we have to set the record straight by not accusing her also of the violation of Church law. The turning point of her life, her "conversion," was occasioned by a severe sickness. The Franciscan confessor took the golden opportunity to speak of hell as well as the ready forgiveness of God.

The new Hyacintha began at thirty to live as a genuine religious. Into a small cell she put only a crucifix and boards for a bed. She no longer received callers. Her corporal penances of atonement were so severe that subsequently the Holy Father noted in the bull of canonization that the very prolongation of her life was a miracle. Apart from her personal need to atone, her strict adherence to the rule became legend. Then, however, as she herself admitted, she had to contend with pride and self-satisfaction, because of her mortifications. "I am punished, but not yet mortified by my sufferings," she once said.

Although women religious could not live today as St.

Hyacintha began, at least within the contemporary structure of religious life, male religious can fall into lax habits, especially with money—such as illicit bank accounts, the appropriation of a personal car, the multiplicity of expensive hobbies, extensive visits and party-going. What does this have to do with the "mortification of the present moment"?

I realize that different communities have varied interpretations of the ordinary ascetics of the religious state. I likewise realize that the superior-general for the whole congregation, the provincial for his province and the local superior for his house, have the duty and right of interpreting the common law. But because a higher superior tolerates woeful laxity out of a misguided concept of peace-keeping, this does not justify violations or give the license to "cut corners." Let everyone look to his own soul. On the day of judgment every man *is* an island, and our rationalizations, subterfuges and presumed permissions will be laid open and smell rotten. Mortification is supposed to cross nature when that nature is in a state of imbalance. It is actually easier to bear the "mortifications of atonement," because they are voluntary, than the "mortifications of the passing moment," because they are involuntary, once we have lost the dedication we professed on the day of vows. Many religious communities have a far greater need of simply observing their Constitutions than a need of up-dating them. But let the members pray that they shall do the former and not omit the latter.

Mortifications of the moment intrude themselves into life by day and by night. The Rule and Constitutions, which impose a tiresome horarium that "forces" us to pray, to study, to work, to travel, when we are disinclined or tired or resentful, is the most important. Then there are the "providential" mortifications that catch us off guard, largely as a result of the ministry assigned to us: the student who is defiant, the parishioner who seeks unwarranted privileges, the unexpected transfer, the unfair assignment, the relative who expects a magic solution to a family problem. These problems are transitory rather than routine. They are significant in this, that their very suddenness is a measure of our self-control. Generally speaking, those religious acquit themselves best in an *unforeseen* circumstance who habitually live in control of themselves by submission to the *routine* of the Rule and Constitutions.

I use the label of "providential" mortifications to underline that God foresees and disposes us by grace to rise to the challenge. Of these challenges the most acute is temptation and unexpected falls into sin. The grace of God to which I refer here is not the obvious grace to overcome sin, nor even the actual grace to rise from sin, but rather the *grace to be calm and confident*, trustful that God will restore us, not discouraged that we have failed, willing to begin anew. A fall into a sin that we have fought for a long time, including deliberate venial sin, is so great a frustration, that it deserves to be included under mortifications of the moment, because, well-understood, it teaches humility, courage and the importance of prayer.

I dislike to subdivide spiritual concepts, because our notions of the spiritual life are complex enough. But I will set down a third category of mortifications of the present moment. We call it community life. Some saints, like the model of seminarians, St. John Berchmans, found community life their serverest mortification. No doubt it is easier to pray alone at times, more satisfying to choose our own television programs, and more peaceful to avoid obnoxious co-religious.

St. John of the Cross, that prince of mystical theologians, in his *Counsels to Religious,* calls our fellow religious the craftsmen sent by God to shape and polish us. Some of them tell us what we dislike hearing and do the contrary things we dislike enduring. Their frustrating and boresome behavior or personality, the saint continues, crosses us and leads us to think others dislike and even despise us. But to survive these annoyances with patience for the love of God and to look upon community life as the place where we are made fit for heaven is a great mortification.

St. John of the Cross was not speaking from theoretical knowledge, but from practical experience. One of the most acute mortifications of the moment—which were anything but momentary for St. John—is misunderstanding from one's co-religious. When he began his reforms of the Carmelites, he was shunned as a "crackpot" upsetting the centuries-old tenor of his order. The better-disposed advised him to leave the country before he gave the community a bad name. The ill-disposed imprisoned him in the Toledo monastery for nine months. Every Friday while he was there, he was scourged on his bare shoulders publicly in the refectory so severely that he bore the scars of the wounds for life. Expelled from the monastery, alone in arid and forbidding terrain, feverish from weakness and desert sun, he chose to go to the monastery at Ubeda, where he knew the superior resented him for a correction St. John gave years earlier, rather than go to the monastery at Baeza, his own foundation, where he might have been at least tolerated. At Ubeda everyone feared to side with such a "criminal." His own confreres, except for a few brothers, seemed to think his downfall and sickness were divine visitations of justice.

We do not have the mortifications of St. John of the Cross to bear, but we do have the same capacity and grace to endure the passing moment of challenge presented by the rule by the horarium, by God's providence, and by our own fellow religious. Patiently endured, it is evidence enough of mortification and assurance sufficient of salvation.

15 : Maturity
in Religious Life

UNTIL THIS POINT I have stressed the attitudes of a religious to his or her environment both inside and outside the cloister: how we must fit into the pattern of our order's apostolate, how we have to bear witness to our profession within the current of human affairs of our own age and nation, how we should react to our co-religious and superiors, and how we must use the "world" to become saints. But transformation into Christ, which is the goal and measure of our effectiveness among men, is a very *personal* thing. I have suggested this repeatedly, but indirectly, in the preceding chapters: that chastity is the relationship that makes God the complement of our personality, that mortification seeks to set our passions and choices in order, that our perseverance in religious life and our growth in holiness depend first of all on accepting ourselves as we are, with all our defects and natural inclinations.

Before we can rightly understand humility and properly orient ourselves to that personal contact with God which is prayer, we need to understand ourselves as *individuals*. Every reaction to God and to the world wherein we operate begins from the attitude we have to ourselves. There is always the danger of too much self-inquiry and accepting the most favorable analysis of our actions, like the dieter on the public scale, whose disappointment at her weight is mollified by the complimentary fortune on the other side of the card.

If there is any natural and supernatural aspect of our lives that reveal us as individuals, it is our emotional life. Some of us are reserved, clipped of speech, somewhat secretive, indifferent to our environment. Others are outgoing, responsive, permissive, even effusive. The thousand combinations of adjectives which describe us as individuals make so many differences in personality possible. These combinations are aligned early in life by those who train us or fail to impress us, and by the many crises that alter our attitudes by upsetting our lives. The important thing which superiors must remember about subjects and all religious about their associations is that *no one is excluded from heaven or is necessarily retarded in spiritual growth because of personality* as long as there is also no question of sinful emotions.

Most psychologists include the whole complex of our intellectual processes, our acts of the will, our passions (in the broader sense of good drives and instincts), and our emotional needs in the general notion of "personality." In this chapter I use the term more restrictively, yet in the popular sense of one's emotional life.

Scripture says that star differs from star in glory, that is, the reward and understanding of the Trinity in heaven varies with the preparation we have made on earth, and no one personality is uniquely acceptable in heaven. The choleric Peter, the impulsive Paul, the affectionate John served God in their individual ways. Did Christ have the "ideal personality?" Say he is rather the ideal *person* whose infused knowledge, unimpeachable holiness and perfect up-bringing in the Holy Family all enabled him to make the best response to every situation in order to fulfill his mission as priest, king and teacher.

I confess that extroverts, jokesters and sanguine persons find small precedent in Christ's historical personality as we see him in the Gospels. Perhaps those biographies were slanted according to the evangelists; perhaps Christ's lighter moments were irrelevant to the purpose of the Gospels. Perhaps his foreknowledge of the passion already in his boyhood moulded him into the "man of sorrows" as a youngster. Some authors have tried to broaden this traditional view of the Master by pointing out he surely smiled as he blessed the children; he surely joked when he called Herod "that fox" and when he agreed with the Samaritan woman that she had no husband. Yet it is obvious that one and the same person cannot continually shift gears and change from introvert to extrovert, from sanguine to melancholic, and so on. It may be that Christ's public life, the main point of the Gospels, had to reflect what the Jews expected of a serious rabbi; hence the Gospels protray him as such a teacher. Scripture scholars emphasize that Christ spoke within the context of the Old Testament and the contemporary devices of using parables and figures of speech. In other words his personal approach to his apostolate was perfectly suited to his times and audience. It is really not necessary, in order to be transformed into Christ, to know any other details, however interesting and helpful they would be. There are many things theologians wish that Christ might have said in the Gospels more clearly, but Tradition must supply our faith.

The significant message of the Gospels for us religious is the *virtues* Christ exemplifies, rather than the *emotional vehicles* of those virtues. Not many religious could become so righteously indignant as to use a belt to drive from a church the ushers taking pew rent during the Mass—as Jesus did to the money-changers, but every religious is obliged to have zeal for the house of God as a house of prayer. Some of the martyrs sang on the way to excruciating tortures and death, as the recently canonized boys from Uganda. Some of the English martyrs cracked jokes before they were beheaded, drawn and quartered, as St. Thomas More and Blessed John Kemble. Yet I would not thereby infer that any of these were braver than Christ, who sweat blood and asked in the Garden that his chalice pass from him.

There is a double point I am making. First, the customs of the religious houses of training imperil the emotional lives of their members by enforcing purely external and pre-conceived emotional patterns of behavior. These religious can expand themselves wholesomely when in the field and out of training, although surely with some regrets and guilty feelings for not conforming. For example, it is purely artificial to demand all the religious to do exactly the same thing together at every recreation and respond with equal warmth to the desires of the leaders of the group. Of course it is important to train young religious to fraternal virtue, but a superior of the young can at times learn as much about fitness of a candidate by observing what that person is likely to do when not coerced to be "loyal" to the group.

There is a second point to be derived from the statement that "putting on Christ" is to imitate his *virtue*, not necessarily those aspects of his human personality foreign to us. Think of all the saints who became transformed into Christ by the end of their lives. What a variety of personalities they represent . . . St. John Bosco's pranks, St. Francis de Sales' suaveness, St. Frances Xavier Cabrini's business sense, St. Therese's child-like affections. Yet they all put on Christ, lived the Christ-life, bore witness to Christ in their corners of the world in four totally different apostolic ways! St. Bernard of Clairvaux, it is said, was so mortified in matters of sight that he did not know who sat across from him in choir nor the subject of the windows in the church. He used to say when some created thing comforted him or delighted him, "I do not dare declare my love of God is ardent." Another saint, Francis of Assisi, took the opposite view and made his delight in the created world a cause of bursts of joy and holy songs. Yet his mortifications and close identification with Christ resulted in the impression of the stigmata, Christ's own wounds in his hands and feet and side. "Star differs from star in glory." Every personality has admission into Paradise.

When a Christian is being transformed into Christ, it is a *person* who changes *morally*. Whereas a religious must also have other qualifications, as health, mental ability and a personality fit for community life and the order's particular works, sanctification depends upon the *will*. The order must accept candidates largely on the grounds of their good-will and increasing ability to grow spiritually in rightly-directed will-power. A summary of *character*, therefore, is a summary of one's virtues. Many religious who are not yet formed spiritually can accomplish a great good in their apostolate because of good-will, just as many "sinless" religious accomplish little because of too small a zeal. In the case of the religious, however, who is either retarded spiritually in himself or who is ineffectual in the apostolate, the lack of progress can often be traced to defects in personality rather than in character. He is not grown-up emotionally. Grace has been unable to build on nature.

Although sanctification looks to morality in the first place, because a *whole person, just as he is,* with strengths and weaknesses, talents and failures, enters religious life, the individual religious will not grow spiritually very much without a proportionate emotional maturity. The variety of saints merely underlines that each *kind* of personality can mature simultaneously on the moral and emotional levels. A frequent condemnation one hears of another member of a community is, "She's a good religious, but no 'ball of fire.'" Although external forms are observed, some quirks of emotion—perhaps moroseness, over-aggressiveness, sentimentalism—prevent that religious from being an integral person. It is controverted among psychologists whether a saint, that is, someone who practices *heroic* virtue, can simultaneously be a neurotic (which is much, much less than the psychotic removed from reality), because a neurosis is a flaw in the emotional makeup. Some would claim that a *saint* (not merely one who is an observant religious) is such an integral person that neurotic flaws would be absent. This is the kind of hypothesis we cannot prove by a statistic or analytical investigation as yet, if ever.

Saintliness would exclude, however, all *excesses* in the emotional life. This, too, is absolutely a personal measure. If the austere St. Bernard who did not look at the windows in church were to have written some of the affectionately emotional letters of St. Therese, it would probably be an excess for him. The difference is more pronounced because they are of different ages and sexes. Each was conditioned in a different childhood milieu— St. Bernard with a number of rough-and-tumble medieval warriors for brothers, and St. Therese with a number of permissive and sensitive older sisters. Yet it would be untrue to say that St. Bernard did not know how to love emotionally; witness his writings on the Mother of God and his exposition of the *Canticle of Canticles*.

Our own age stresses individual liberty: democratic election of officers, freedom of conscience to worship as a minority, racial and national struggles for independence. Hence in religious life, too, we shall see an increasing amount of individual self-expression, emotional freedom, the assignment of religious according to their natural bents and inclinations. It will not be easy for an old community to adjust its customs to these concepts of freedom. But, as is always true in the history of religious orders, the individual must look to his own sanctity and emotional stability. Freedom to express our emotional lives by more contacts with our family, by satisfying creative and artistic urges, by identifying ourselves with the misery of the poor and under-privileged, requires individual self-control. Because we have no way to measure emotional maturity or fully to identify what might be an excess in one religious and not another, a great deal of charity is required in our judgments of each other.

The individual religious must see if the *signs* of emotional maturity are present in his life. In all times and at all ages, of course, the traditional modes of religious' emotional behavior are necessarily present in a saintly person: a placid, calm acceptance of what is inevitable, the happiness and satisfaction in doing what we know is valuable, the hopeful trust that our problems will ultimately resolve themselves, the confidence in ourselves to cope with daily professional problems. These *natural* emotions are expressions of the mature spiritual and moral life of a religious; hence we see how the above signs, which are present even in non-believers, are the emotional supports of spiritual growth. Although it is possible to have minimal *natural* emotional maturity independently of religion, *this is not verified in the lives of religious, whose very failures in spiritual life occasion emotional upheavals.* Therefore it is important to understand ourselves.

Unfortunately age is no guarantee of emotional growth, precisely because our spiritual life is such a factor in emotional maturity. I said in a previous chapter that a great need of every religious order is the example of older members who are placid, gracious, approachable models of observance, that is, who combine emotional and spiritual maturity. It is depressing to younger members to see the worst exhibitions of childish behavior in older religious of their community. But the following examples are not restricted to older religious.

As a child won't play in a game unless it's on his terms, some religious won't accept assignments unless on their terms. As a child throws a tantrum when scolded, some religious defy superiors who reprimand them. As a child interprets it as a deliberate personal injury when the weather, business of the parents or sickness inhibits it, some religious complain endlessly about things over which they have no control. As the child who leads a game demands to make all the rules of play, some religious superiors take it as a personal affront when their subjects disobey a rule. As a child impulsively wishes death or dire tragedy on those who cross it, some religious, while not wishing for such tragedies, see in them the opportunity for their own advancement and ambitions. As a child runs from opposition, some religious avoid the adult and amicable way of settling differences by confrontation. As a child calls a stronger enemy names, some religious resort to labels and epithets applied to those who are their intellectual and spiritual superiors. As a child is wary and suspicious of strangers and new situations, some religious shy away from every change in policy, liturgy or personnel. As a child broods in a corner to attract sympathy for its failures, some religious act like martyrs to attract sympathy for the ills they bring upon themselves. And most common of all, as a child exaggerates its bruises and pains out of proportion, some religious become hypochondriacs either to divert attention from their lack of zeal, to cover up their spiritual disabilities, or to win the sympathy and indulgence of their co-religious as well as lay persons. A continual justification that must be made for the laziness or culpable ineptitude of a confrere in the house is, "Father (or sister or brother) would do so much more, but he (or she) has been sick." Or the belabored, "He (or she) is a good religious, but hasn't been feeling well lately."

No one should fear emotion in religion. Not only is it a legitimate aspiration of holy feelings, but *an integral personality uses his emotions to energize* the decisions of his will. There is no substitute for enthusiasm, fear of offending God, energetic convictions and all the other emotional overtones of religious acts. In fact, the Scripture cites joy and peace and happiness as the consequences of virtue. Men particularly, both in religious life and out of it, are reluctant to express emotions of a religious nature, even though they are often very demonstrative of social

emotions of fellowship and good cheer. This is unfortunate for their preaching and counseling. The stifled emotions and lack of sympathy of some sisters likewise hurt
their apostolate. Our feelings are not evil. The fact that
emotions are partly mental states and partly physical re-
actions make it possible for us to integrate all our personal resources for the apostolate. Feelings are meant by
God to be the springboard of actions. I have never actually seen any example of purely mental or intellectual love.
True love is a complex affair, including aversion and attraction and sentiment and desire for good and even the
physical sensations—however slight—of well-being,
quickened pulse at times and apparently the operation of
some glands as well. This is not a depreciation of the spiritual qualities of love, including the love of a religious for
God, but an encouragement to use our whole person to
seek God with maturity on every level of life. Perhaps
that is what the Old Testament phrase quoted by Christ
really meant: "You shall love the Lord your God with
your whole mind, your whole soul, and your whole
strength." This is the first and greatest emotion in religious lives.

16 : "Be Not Wise in Your Own Conceit"

Spiritual writers have a way of making whatever virtue they are writing about particularly important. Thus prudence is the queen of virtues because it regulates the others; charity is the crown of virtues because love is the greatest commandment; justice is the all-inclusive virtue, because it renders to God, our neighbor and ourselves what is due; voluntary poverty is the most Christ-like virtue because it gives us an external resemblance to Jesus. But I think the writers have a point when they make humility the foundation of all the virtues, because self-knowledge is necessary to see the sins and imperfections that hinder our growth in all the virtues.

Humility is also the most elusive virtue to define. Because it is a cognate of "humiliation," and because both words derive from the Latin term for "earth" or "ground," there is a popular misconception that the humble person seeks humiliation and has a low-down opinion of what he is capable of accomplishing. Apart from the fact that his description also fits psychotic personalities, enough of it is true to obscure what is false. The humble person is down-to-earth, but not necessarily an earthly and unsophisti-

cated person. On the other hand, great learning, high
church position and distinction in one's apostolate are not
guarantees of sanctity; in fact, these qualities often mili-
tate against the foundation of sanctity we call humility.
This is attested to by those saints who eschewed offices
and university degrees. Nevertheless, the challenge to remain humble despite distinctions is a wonderful opportunity to be at once a leader in the Church and a submis-
sive tool in God's hands. The history of the Church shows
us that even the highest offices, degrees and talents do
not exclude humility. In fact, everything else being equal,
the man of talent, because of superior insights, and the
man in a high position, because of the grace of office,
ought to make even greater progress in humility in the
midst of the opportunities to practice this virtue. Conversely, a man of inferior spiritual abilities had better
pray fervently when greatness is thrust upon him through
offices, distinctions and degrees.

Be he great in the Church or insignificant in its external operations—for anyone on earth might be the holiest
and therefore the most important cog in the Church's internal processes—everyone has a certain number of pretensions: an extensive vocabulary, a wealthy background,
much travel, being sought out for spiritual direction,
"name-dropping" of the great persons whose light reflects
through him, social graces that make him shine in public
functions, dynamic delivery in the pulpit, a resonant
voice at worship, dexterity in some sport, wittiness expected of him at parties, skill in maintaining motors,
plumbing and the television, and, above all, the memory
to be able to quote from appropriate mystical authors on
any topic named. Who can lift his head after even such a
partial list? The damnable thing is that these pretensions

are generally true, for the most part, hence they hang on to life as long as we do.

Let us use the notion of emotional maturity as our starting point. Humility sees and accepts its limitations, even as it admits its talents and graces. Sometimes it is tiresome and puzzling to hear the saints beat their breasts and confess they are terrible sinners, when it seems as if they should admit their talents and graces. After all, did they not arrive at their holy estate by exercise in virtue and long hours of prayer? The answer is that the saints saw all the graces, especially in their fledgling days, which they did not use without reserve. That is why St. Teresa of Avila said anyone who refused God *nothing* for six months could be a great saint. That is why St. Francis could point to a criminal or sinner and say he would be in similar straits, but for the grace of God. The devout soul knows there is always a little more he could have done, a little further he could have pressed himself. Thus humility, or knowledge of self, causes us to assess sin not only by the God offended, but also by the graces rejected. The greater awareness of God in their souls by sanctifying grace made slighter sins loom large to the saints. So we might "agree" with the humble saints claiming they were sinful, not by reason of the magnitude of their imperfections, but by reason of the adumbration of the Christ-life in their bodies and souls—apart from what may have been the history of their earlier falls.

It may even be a comfort to know that no saint is born; they are all made, notwithstanding those who allegedly abstained in babyhood from their mother's milk on Wednesdays and Fridays in Lent! Blessed Angela of Foligno, a Franciscan tertiary sister, admitted that she wanted a great reputation for sanctity as a young religious. She would like to have guests in the house see her fast and abstain at table. She even tried to edify them by her poor bed after she had hidden the extra blankets. St. Vincent de Paul was already the founder of a flourishing congregation, had a reputation for counseling and had established caritative works in many areas of France, when he was suddenly tempted to have pretensions. He had on a few occasions earlier been embarrassed when his classmates saw his peasant father with him in public. Now he shrank when it was announced that his awkward and poorly-clad nephew from the country was waiting to see him. He had already told the porter to bring the lad up secretly by a private staircase when he realized his weakness and ran after the porter to amend his order. The saint expiated this trivial fall—great to him—by introducing the boy as a typical member of his family to all the members of the household. The fact that this is not a legend is proved by the witness of his confreres at the next annual retreat, who heard St. Vincent ask pardon of the whole congregation for deluding them into thinking he was a great saint. Even the redoubtable St. John of the Cross had to acquire humility somewhat painfully. After he completed his theological course with distinction, he was quite impossible to live with in the monastery, for he seemed to have an opinion on everything. His spiritual director ordered him to forsake his profound books for some time and just use a child's catechism for spiritual reading and reflection. Thus St. John learned that every man, including those without theological training, had access to the basic faith that leads to sanctity.

"Do not seek for what is above your head," Sirach tells us, "and do not search for what exceeds your ability."

Even profound theologians can apply what the Scriptures seem to direct only to unlettered souls. No one should acquire knowledge, even of God, if it is only to flaunt it to our co-religious or write books that will reap some harvest of money and fame. Then that knowledge *is* above our heads to assimilate and *does* exceed our capacity to use it for a proper apostolate and self-sanctification. We cannot be said to "seek," however, if *obedience* imposes the acquisition of degrees and the attending of conferences and meetings upon us. The religious who requests these things had better be sure of his motives. One praiseworthy motive for advancement in studies is to bring prestige to one's community—this is loyalty; another worthwhile motive is the usefulness of knowledge for a future apostolate—this is proper zeal. The most important reason of all for advanced studies (or for hobby-crafting or for mortification or for humility itself) is one's own sanctification.

Knowledge, like everything else in the world except sin, is a stepping-stone to God. All ideas and possible ideas exist first of all in God; methaphysics tells us that there is no division in God, hence his ideas and his beauty and his goodness and his power are *co-terminous* with his divine Self. Hence every time we learn a little, improve a little, love a little more, we get a more complete picture of God. Of course it is merely a natural picture unless it is related to the grace within us. It may be, as some philosophers claim, that knowledge is an end in itself, but for a religious whose self-acknowledged end is union with God, all knowledge leads to God or away from him. This is not to imply the only legitimate knowledge for us is theological; this is surely an anti-intellectual and anti-human attitude. I have observed religious receive insights from reading great poetry, work off depression or anger banging a piano or a hammer, discover the needs of laymen by reading fine books, and win good influence over the young through knowledge of sports. Therefore when we develop our talents, humility directs that we are mindful of our calling and the One who has called us.

In the chapter on mortification I emphasized that pride is a good drive, as all the "passions" are good. Sin and defect gain entrance into our souls when we tolerate excess. For example, one ought to be proud he is God's friend in the state of grace, but it is an excess to see himself smugly as well along the road to holiness, as worthy of being consulted in spiritual problems because of his supposed experience, or as exemplifying serenity, gravity, edification and other merely external forms of religion. Whereas we are obliged to aim for such a pattern of behavior, its existence is not a necessary sign of interior virtue, particularly if we strive for these external appearances, as many younger religious, in a spirit of envious rivalry and unholy emulation. This arises from the exaggerated regard we have for ourselves and our egotistical desire to appear "pious" in our own eyes—the basest form of self-deception. One real sign of humility is to admit the existence of a virtue in others without regret, that they possess what we have such a tiresome task in acquiring.

What I have really been driving at during these paragraphs is to say humility is not depreciating ourselves, but rightly appreciating what God has given us. We can take the next logical step and show that mature humility does not bother either to deny its abilities or to flaunt them or even to think about them. Humility is too wrapped up in God to get excited about itself one way or the other. Except for those ever-present pretensions, I believe most religious acquire this indifference to themselves in time, but it is not easy to distinguish what is genuine humility and what is merely laxity. St. Margaret of Cortona asked the Lord why he lavished such spiritual favors on her, "such dust and ashes, filth and darkness," after her life of debauchery. Christ replied that he searched through the bottom of the world's abyss and chose her precisely because it is his way and his pleasure to "exalt the humble, justify sinners and change what is vile into something precious." If every religious realized that a vocation is largely just that for most of us, there would not be many proud religious left in the world. It is easy to make ourselves into tin gods on low platforms, because the laity respect our cloth even when we soil it. But we have no right, as a result of this respect, to "play god:" to dominate conversations and thrust our opinions on others; to justify our actions as if, like God, we could do no wrong; to compare our superior qualities with others and decry their inefficiency and slower rate of learning; to be "bossy" and critical when circumstances place us in charge of others.

Christ is very clear. "Without me you can do nothing." And elsewhere, "What do you have that you have not received?" The ornaments of a priest, brother, and sister—in so far as they are *religious*, not just other human beings—are not social graces, degrees, positions, friends, talents, or even the religious garb. Their glory and ornament is to reflect the life of Christ in their own environment. This is the Christ who humbled himself and did not think it demeaned him to appear in the guise of a creature, but was even obedient to the death of the cross.

Only God actually knows how closely we have achieved this Christ-life; our worth is only what God sees us to be. The opponents of Christianity scoff at what they call our "servile status" and sneer that the hierarchy keeps us in such servitude to bolster their power. If these opponents of the Church knew the Christ who was crowned with thorns and mocked for a fool and killed as a divine impostor, they would not laugh at our genuflections, our voluntary humiliations and our frequent confession of sin.

There is a two-sided yardstick to gauge our humility in the sense of self-knowledge bringing us to closer union with God. This yardstick also links humility with emotional maturity. One side of the yardstick is calibrated by our values, the other by our long-range goals. Our values are identifiable by the things we dream about and hope for—being a missionary, teacher, laboratory technician in a hospital. Our values lie in the things we are interested in most and what commands our attention above all else— God or sports, breviary or the newscast, our convenience or the good of souls. Maturity of emotion and awareness of our fundamental relationship with God—or humility —prompts us to erect a value-system, standards of excellence in our choices and a hierarchy of importance. We can make constructive choices and responsible decisions. For example, to dream of glorious (self-centered) martyrdom, a far-fetched eventuality, is neither mature nor humble, particularly if we complain about the weather or run for the tranquillizers. It is the wrong hierarchy of values and evidence of the absence of humility to be concerned about a receding hairline, or what our students or parishioners may say about us when we have done the best we can. As a final example, our relationship with

God and our humility are askew, if we attempt to catch the eye or ear of others by singularity in the community due to our ecstatic genuflections, our collection of relics, our personal affectations in public prayer, the "special" way we wear the religious habit.

The other side of the yardstick, I said, is respect for our long-range goals, which is whatever contributes to our spiritual maturity and an effective apostolate. The gauge is action, not words. There is no point to asserting that heaven is our true home, and repeatedly skipping or culpably sleeping during meditation, which provides the contact that leads us to God. A spiritually perceptive man develops a humble awareness that he needs patience to achieve his long-range goals. For example, we accept correction even if it rankles us because of the manner in which it was administered. To seethe or plot inwardly betrays our pride and inability to see the usefulness of correction. On the positive side we are grateful for all favors, not only from God, but from those who teach us the techniques and facts we need as priests, brothers, or sisters. I am never worried about the ultimate victory of humility in even the religious who have some small pretensions and self-delusions when I see them laughing at their foibles, weaknesses and vanities, their age, their weight and their baldness. They have learned to ask with the saints, *Quid hoc ad aeternitatem?*—"How does this count for eternity?"

17 : Spiritual Reading: Profit and Loss

KNOWLEDGE of God and ourselves comes from reading and hearing. The resolutions and aspirations of our mental prayer have the same obvious source. Physically we become what we feed upon. Mentally we become what we assimilate through our senses. Besides listening to the word of God being preached and explained, the chief resource of the spiritual life that we can provide of ourselves is spiritual reading. It is an important means of counteracting the diet of secular magazines, novels, newspapers, or even letters, because we are prone to think about what we read. I believe one of the more important tasks of a superior is to choose table reading with great care. Few religious have the time to page through magazines and weekly newspapers for relevant articles. Instead of choosing a dry or profound or technical book to do battle with clanking forks and rattling plates, the superior ought to mark articles to be read in common. The light and popular approach of a periodical is more likely to hold the listeners' interest anyway. Otherwise a truly great spiritual book may be truly useless when read in the wrong environment. Religious are called upon to comment on so many local and world situations, but they lose chances to form others' opinions because they are themselves ignorant—often through no fault of their own.

The very book you are now reading is a poor one to read at table. It might be suitable for spiritual reading in common where that is the practice. It can serve as a supplemental text for training young religious, if they are given a chance to ask questions. It can serve as the basis of discussion periods or question-and-answer sessions at a retreat or renewal program. Perhaps it can serve as a sourcebook for those who preach to or counsel religious. But the chief purpose of a book like this, with which the annual market is flooded, is to clarify concepts, garner some new insights, or reject the opinions of the author —but as a book for private spiritual reading. As I shall point out later, just because something appears in print, it does not have the validity of the Gospel.

As a meditation book is chosen according to one's capacity and need, so the spiritual reading material must be neither too high nor too low, but in our own key. On the other hand, such a book is not to be chosen for its ability to divert us; some of the most profitable ones require concentration and re-reading and note-taking. What is pietistic and flowery is not likely to ground one in theology. Yet a book, even a rather difficult book, in one of the branches of theology, does more to generate true piety and feed the mind for prayer than a dozen "devotional" books that repeat what has been written for a thousand years. It is so important to seek a rational and Scriptural foundation for our convictions. It is better to dig a catechism or basic *tyrocinium* out of the library and mull over it for a month of spiritual reading than pore over a newsletter from some shrine about the latest apparition and miracles and sensational occurrences. There is a place for the latter in the Church, if the source is as well-proven as Lourdes or Fatima. But we also have the unfortunate events that are better left unmentioned at this time. Religious who become involved in weeping Madonnas, bleeding crucifixes and voices in the night are trying to fly before they have learned to walk. Not only do they discredit their calling and betray a weakness in their training, but they lead others astray and often substitute hysteria for solid and unequivocal piety. As for those who circulate even true stories about cases of possession, let them beware of trifling with the affairs of Satan without the Church's authorization. The super-intelligence of the devil may induce a few fixations of their own in the minds of the morbidly curious.

Even the writings of saints and holy persons challenge our discrimination. I am not here referring to the theological opinions that the Church may subsequently have condemned; the opinion was surely tenable when proposed, as, for instance, the erroneous opinions about the essence of the Mass. Nor am I referring to the descriptions of heaven, hell, or events of Christ's and Mary's lives that we can find in the revelations of some of the saints and blesseds. These latter can be good meditations, but they cannot all be accurate, since the details of Christ's and Mary's lives, for example, vary in the works of St. Brigid of Sweden, St. Catherine Emmerich and Ven. Mary Agreda. It would be ignorant to condemn what pontiffs and bishops have approved as being without heresy. There is no guarantee, however, that the contradictory accounts of mystics are all true. An *imprimatur* is negative approval. How does one otherwise account for contradictions in the saints' writings? We must remember that everything a person perceives, he perceives according to his previous conditioning. As an African artist protrays an African Madonna, so a mystic has insights and visions according to his background. One might "see" the Crucified with three nails, another with four, according to some crucifix familiar from childhood. It is nothing to get excited about, even though we wish we knew every detail of Christ's passion.

Another factor we ought to remember is that we cannot take a sentence or paragraph from a writer and magnify it out of proportion. Many authors, when they desire to emphasize a point (as the examples toward the end of this chapter will demonstrate), support it with so many arguments, that we lose sight of other relevant points. For example, I have heard it said by competent theologians that one can "prove" half a dozen heresies from the works of St. Augustine. He emphasized different aspects of grace and free-will when he fought Pelagians, Semi-Pelagians and Manichaeans. Martin Luther quoted from St. Augustine frequently. In the same vein one can find suspicions of heretical Quietism and obscurantism in such a time-honored phrase from the *Imitation of Christ* as, "I would rather feel compuction rather than know how to define it." I have already considered the dictum, "Every time I have gone out among men I have come back less a man." Many a Franciscan spiritual director has cautioned his charges against a too-literal interpretation of *The Little Flowers of St. Francis*—for example, those passages that see intellectual learning as "possessions of the mind." I remember one novice who brought in St. John of the Cross to his novice-master for an explanation and was told to return it to the library and withdraw *David Copperfield* for the next month's spiritual reading.

An important apostolic reason why religious and priests have to use their theological training for the selection, reading and interpretation of spiritual books is that the sanctification of others depends upon our own. The blind cannot lead the blind. Astigmatic vision from the gullible reading of sensational, profoundly mystical, or one-sided authors, which I have described, is all the more dangerous for being partially correct. Theological students should read and have interpreted for them the works of St. John of the Cross, but they can develop many problems because of its literary form and their own lack of mystical experience by which to comprehend the saint concretely. Nor can one be ignorant of the terms of scholastic faculty psychology.

The medievals used to say, *contemplata aliis tradere,* "pass along to others what has struck you." According to each religious' apostolate or convictions he should savor and reflect upon his reading, then commit salient points to a notebook or file card. This can serve as a source for preaching and teaching, or simply as a means of recalling useful spiritual facts or well-turned phrases to aid one's own growth in grace. It is true, however, that spiritual reading and mental prayer are not the times to write a sermon or a religion class. But the Spirit breathes when and where he wills, and it is a loss to oneself and others to lose an insight that may never return to us, because we failed to pencil a note in margin of a book or inscribe it in ink in a notebook. Every book deserves the courtesy of methodical reading. There is always a temptation to read difficult matter superficially. To read a currently fashionable or controversial author merely to say we have done so, or to drop a few obscure quotations during conversation is ridiculous and proud.

What shall we read? Because religious read the Scriptures during Mass or a few verses at the beginning of meals or at other times of the day, they tend to slight the reading of Scriptures as regular fare. St. Jerome warns us, "Ignorance of the Scriptures is ignorance of Christ." St. Francis once separated the pages of the New Testament and distributed them among his friars, so that they might each possess a fragment of the word of God. Those who were unlettered were instructed to carry the page in a pocket over the heart. Just as important as the indulgenced reading of the Bible is the reading of commentaries and explanations of the background. We actually know more about the Old Testament today from collateral literature than the scholars of the early Church. As for the New Testament, there is a short-coming in the training of religious who cannot explain to non-Catholic objectors the meaning of such phrases as, "the brothers and sisters of Jesus," "Mary brought forth her first-born son," "What is that to you, woman?" and so forth. To those apostolic religious who make themselves accessible to conversation in trains and planes such questions are inevitable.

After the Bible our own Rule and Constitutions are high on the list of spiritual books. For us they are the marrow of the Gospel and the key to heaven, for if we faithfully observe them, we are *guaranteed* heaven. What is more relevant than being reminded of our promises, our customs, our rights, our objectives, and our reward in eternal life?

In our own time we have seen the publication of lives of the saints in books whose viewpoint represent a departure from older hagiography. The lives of saints seem always to have been a source of "conversions"—even to

other future saints, if we recall St. Ignatius Loyola.
Therefore there is no point in disparaging the many centuries of spiritual biographies that relied so heavily on
legend, continual miracles, exaggerations of mystical experiences and disproportionate emphasis on corporal penance and ecstasies. These stories are not necessarily true,
but they are not necessarily false, either. Very often the
bulls of canonization cite these factors as evidence of
heroic sanctity and we cannot lightly brush them aside as
fantasy. But I am referring to the "superman" concept
discernible in the lives of some past saints. A case in
point is St. Francis of Assisi. St. Bonaventure, as the minister general of the order, was commissioned, as it were,
to write the biography of St. Francis. Since many friars
were yet alive who had witnessed the foundation of the
order, St. Bonaventure questioned them and recorded
their eye-witness accounts on paper. Then, because of the
spurious tales of those who were separatist groups in the
community, he unsuccessfully attempted to have other
biographies destroyed. However, even when his authentic
history of the founder was circulated, the membership
was dissatisfied because there were too few miracles and
some of the popular and currently sensational stories
were absent. So the minister general had to write a second history which included these tales.

Today, however, critical scholarship has given us a
kind of a hagiography that is at once more revelatory of
the whole saint and more in agreement with the spirit of
our scientific age. Modern stories balance our impractical
notions of sanctity. They point out the slow growth of
sanctity and the flaws of character that preceded growth
in holiness. We can read saints' letters, the comments of
their contemporaries, and official chronicles. We even

have snapshots of the more recent saints that show they are peasants, or unglamorous, or even able to smile. Some have objected to this supposedly untraditional biography of a saint, but their objections crumble under our ability to identify more closely with the heroes of the Church. It is spiritually profitable to see them practical, down-to-earth and joking, and not only as idealist dreamers—although they were that, too.

I have leveled many general criticisms against some types of spiritual reading in the hope that religious take a more realistic and intellectual point of view. I would like to review some specific cases which can serve as examples of unbalanced viewpoints.

(1) Because of pride in one of her works, God took consolations away from Blessed Clare of Montefalco. Despite her tears, penance and use of the discipline *for fifteen years* in an effort to win them back, it was useless. *Comment*: Either the single act of pride was a terrible sin or God is singularly unjust in this story. In any event we cannot approve of the attachment of the person in the story to her consolations and trying to "buy" them back from God with tears and blood.

(2) In order to get more abuse from her family St. Rose of Lima not only did not excuse herself from their accusations, but even exaggerated things, so that they would think she deserved punishment. *Comment*: A psychiatrist would have a field day with a story of an unmarried young woman telling lies to get punished. St. Rose was such a wonderful saint that we do not have to slant her life with untruth. Unfortunately these vignettes are generally cited in support of one factor in spiritual life to the exclusion of others and hence are printed out of their context.

3) Sister Joan Mary of the Blessed Trinity *never* satisfied any of her inclinations. She *always* chose what was most uncomfortable and displeasing to her. *Comment*: This is an admirable sentiment, but it reflects the level of mature life. Hence, without explanation, it can discourage young religious. In the chapter on mortifications I pointed out the spiritual danger of endlessly trying to cross nature as if it were evil in itself.

(4) St. Basil asked an abbot if any monk showed greater evidence of sanctity than the rest. The abbot introduced him to a simple brother. St. Basil knelt and washed the humble monk's feet, and the latter offered no protest. Because of the monk's obedience, the next morning St. Basil came into the church and without warning *ordained* the still unresisting monk to the priesthood. *Comment*: Such a simplistic concept of "blind" obedience is a matter requiring training and positive consent can only obscure the real nature of the vows and the rationality of our faith. Once more, there may be circumstances that could color this story favorably, but none are provided in this story.

(5) St. Francis of Assisi was careful to observe the prescribed hours of prayer. In December, 1223, returning from Rome, he stopped to say his breviary; he stood in the rain and got soaked through (the story goes). *Comment:* A popular folk-saying has it that even a dog knows when to come in out of the rain. By 1223 St. Francis was already suffering from a number of ailments. The December rain was no help. By emphasizing the importance of the time for prayer, the author approves of sidestepping common sense in the spiritual life. Nor does the author avert to the damage done to the breviary written

in ink, an expensive item in the thirteenth century, especially for the Poverello of Assisi!

(6) Brother Juniper, an early Franciscan brother, was reprimanded by his superior for his too great generosity in giving an alms. In the middle of the night Juniper rose and served the superior, whom he had awakened, a bowl of porridge with a lump of butter, adding the comment that he had noticed the superior's voice was hoarse with excitement during the reprimand. When the superior understandably raised his voice again, Juniper asked him to hold the light while *he* ate the porridge, since it was cooked already. The tale ends with the "conversion" of the superior. *Comment:* I would send Brother Juniper away for a month's retreat.

18 : Public Prayers
and Private Sentiments

DURING THE REIGN of the Manchu Emperors of China, the officials devised an elaborate ritual to sequester their rulers from the populace. Even important dignitaries and ambassadors were subjected to lengthy procedures at court. Of these the "kowtow" was the proper show of respect to the emperor. Protocol required everyone who approached to kneel three times and touch the forehead to the floor three times at each genuflection. But the imperial court did not reckon with American democracy. The U.S. government sent John E. Ward to negotiate a trade treaty with China in 1859. Because he refused to submit to the kowtow, Ward learned the trade agreement was impossible. But the Chinese, desirous of the alliance, tried to compromise. Would Ward at least appear to stumble and quickly kowtow at least once to "save face"? No, Ward would not, since he knelt only to God and a woman to propose marriage. Would Ward shield himself with a table and hold on to it while making a quick kowtow? No, indeed. Not even a simple bow from the waist? And so on and on.

I forget how this tiresome bit of diplomacy ended. But

when I think of the "liturgies" demanded by society in diplomacy, in courtship, in cocktail-drinking and in courtroom procedures, I am astounded at Christians who balk at the protocol surrounding the worship of the one, true God. It is a good practice for men, who are a composite of a visible body and invisible soul, to surround the virtues of patriotism, business arrangements and civil ceremonies with display and ritual that externalize their sentiments. How can we do less for divine worship according to that same, integral human nature? In the same vein, just as an *individual* assumes postures for prayer and fixes his attention upon concrete objects to give *integral* human worship, *groups of men*—whether in parishes, convents or the field of battle—offer *social* worship to the Creator. To genuflect, to wash oneself symbolically with holy water, to fast an hour before the Eucharist are courtesies we observe as members of a Catholic society.

Because religious are especially consecrated to the service of God and already form units within the Mystical Body, their collective expression of dependence upon God through liturgy should have particular exactitude and be an example to the less-closely united members of a parish, who regularly meet only once a week in common worship. When the religious—whatever their status as seminary groups, teaching sisters or brothers, or religious priests with the care of souls—join the parish congregation for worship, their background and training can make the liturgy more meaningful for the laity. Once more personal sanctification has an apostolic outlet. Far from avoiding such a Sunday contact (or at times of special services) religious should welcome this opportunity for fellowship and the chance to bear witness to their Christ-life in public. It is a sad day for the Church when conservative superiors, both of men and women, either apply new directives unwillingly or defy the wishes of the Holy See by not implementing its decrees under spurious titles of exemption—at least in their own houses. Instead of leading the laity (at least as exemplars where the religious have no care of souls) and supporting the bishop and diocesan clergy, some religious drag their feet as if a bishop's directive were possibly a matter for further discussion. Even if the very diocesan clergy themselves were slow to carry out liturgical reforms, it is not the role of religious to hesitate, but to pioneer. At least let us hope the houses of training of religious congregations will provide an up-dated training in the meaning and execution of liturgical prayer.

There are times when every Christian would rather pray alone, perhaps in chapel, perhaps on a mountain top or on a seashore. When you pray alone, it is a member of the Church at prayer; when you pray the official liturgy, it is the Church herself at prayer. Without dwelling on the ancient Greek origin of the word to describe the service of an individual to the state, "liturgy" has the radical meaning of "the work of the people" or "the public endeavor." Therefore Christ tells us whenever two or more of his disciples gather in his name, he is present among them. During liturgical services he speaks to us from the Scriptures, he is spoken of during the sermon or homily, he stands in the person of the priest to offer our reverence to the Father and our suffrages for mankind, he gives himself to us in the Eucharist, and he abides in us when we leave through the increase of the divine life, which we call sanctifying grace. Further, because the liturgy, including the Divine Office, mirrors the mysteries of the Lord, we are urged to reflective imitation in our Christ-life. Adequately understood and practiced in concrete terms of daily life, liturgical prayer would probably suffice to make us saints without any additional vocal prayers. It would spark our meditations all day and prompt us to frequent aspirations. The Mass, Scriptural readings and the Psalms were the ordinary and sufficient vocal prayer of the Church for centuries. I believe the best para-liturgical prayers of any Christian are eminently those linked to public worship. The point of liturgical prayer is to be the common starting point of all Christians, because "as we pray, so do we believe." In other words the dogmatic and moral truths by which we live are underscored in the liturgy. In the first liturgy of the Church, this public prayer was precisely the means of instructing the faithful—vernacular Scripture, the homily interpreting the mysteries of Christ-among-us, greater group participation in administering the sacraments, the "prayer of the faithful" to involve every Christtian in the expression of particular needs of the day, and an appreciation of the symbolism and signs of the sacramentals. The more complex ratiocinations of medieval theology and the subtler details of morality, of course, cannot be taught by the liturgy, which rather buttresses our fundamental faith. In any case, liturgy, since it is a common starting point, should be the raw material, the matrix, the springboard of private prayer. Even the loftiest flights of the mystics were occasioned by participation in the Mass and the reading of Scriptures, which yet today chiefly comprise the Divine Office.

Many religious seem to consider their daily community worship a burdensome routine. To participate in the responses and learn to sing in a group seems to them merely a framework for private prayer—to finish the prayers and songs in common as painlessly and as briefly as possible to satisfy precept, so they can "really start praying," as during the Offertory, after the Sanctus and at Communion time. Some wish to get in their favorite prayers; major seminarians have to "catch up" on their breviary; others want to say the rosary they foresee they will have no time for later in the day. Their singing is sluggish, and the choir director is the enemy of their souls! It seems to me that, whereas religious orders generally have over-developed systems of meditation and community vocal prayers of the non-liturgical kind, they have no well-defined sense of *liturgical* piety. I remember the humorous—or perhaps humorless—tale of the monks who stopped the Divine Office during a cataclysmic storm in order to pray for divine assistance! The burden of this paragraph and the whole chapter is not to derogate from other vocal prayers nor to neglect meditation nor to throw out the Rosary. On the contrary, these exercises ought to receive increased meaning when the religious share in the annual unfolding of the liturgy. But the fact that liturgy is *official* prayer was never meant to imply merely external forms and the trappings of worship.

I venture to say that historically—whether of Church decree or as the result of a revelation received by a saint —most of the extra-liturgical prayers in the Raccolta are the popular response to the spiritual needs of the faithful. Many of the prayers are merely *vernacular* excerpts from the Mass and Divine Office, to which particular indulgences were attached. I believe, however, it is an extreme and unwarranted view on the part of some liturgists who believe that the adoption of new feasts into the liturgy and into popular, extra-liturgical prayer-forms, such as novenas and Benediction, was merely a sop to satisfy a desire on the part of the people of God to replace with comprehensible prayer-forms what they no longer understood in the Mass. On the contrary, the addition of feasts that popularize devotion to the mysteries of Christ and Mary—as the Sacred Heart, Forty Hours, the Immaculate Conception—should be interpreted as the natural evolution of Church worship throughout the centuries. If history can verify that the true and proper expressions of worship were lost to the Church about the fourth century because of heresies and the intricate maze of Eastern forms of worship, it seems to be a negative commentary on the effectiveness of Divine providence in the all-important area of official prayer for sixteen hundred years. There is no simple answer, perhaps, but every development in the liturgy should be interpreted according to the needs of its own century, not of our times. For example, the tenth and sixteenth centuries, which suffered notable liturgical setbacks according to our contemporary viewpoint, due to heresies and the secularistic papacy, were also outstanding periods of missionary expansion, something of a proof of vitality in the Mystical Body.

I have made this footnote to history in the light of the statement of Pope Pius XII that mere antiquity is not an absolute criterion in the restoration or promotion of liturgical forms. The Stations of the Cross is an example of a non-liturgical prayer. Its present status is not very old, having developed from divergent forms under the Franciscans until it was stabilized in the sixteenth century. Some of the stations have no reliable historical source and the route pointed out to pilgrims in Jerusalem itself underwent many variations. Yet particularly when made alone from place to place, the Stations of the Cross are a fruitful meditation and derive chiefly from the Scriptures.

It would be retrogression to delete this expression of Christian piety simply because there is no precedent for it in the catacombs. I imagine a Bible Vigil derived from the Good Friday liturgy, including lamentations, reading the Passion and venerating the Crucified, would be as spiritually fruitful, especially during Lent, but that is not how Catholic prayer-life has developed. There is room for both to exist side by side with the official liturgy. Religious orders of men and women have been the traditional depository and vehicle of these non-liturgical prayers. They should continue to foster what is consonant with the mind of the Church even as they should stand in front by their obedience to the latest decrees on liturgy.

A most concrete example is the sensitive area of novenas. We cannot omit to mention that the Apostles prepared for the Holy Spirit by a novena. Hence the novena has an important Scriptural precedent. But a novena of Masses or Bible Vigils with relevant homilies might be the best preparation to understand the mysteries of Christ and his mother and the saints. In other words, the para-liturgical service must reinforce our understanding of Catholic doctrine. To pray for nine days or nine weeks or nine First Fridays is, after all, not an evil thing. It is just that the format, sentimental hymns and prayers which lack appeal to the intellect and do not demand acts of the will to change our lives are not the most fruitful means of common prayer. We should make the liturgy, not excluding the sermon, the standard of excellence for all other expressions of Catholic prayer-life.

Just as this applies to the Church at large and to those religious communities dedicated to particular mysteries of Christianity, so the individual religious have now been given a mandate by the bishops of the world to conform their own prayer-life to the liturgy. Those communities who recite the full breviary can also use the breviary passages for meditation in common, whether formally as explained in a supplemental text, or individually according to inspiration. The prayers of the Mass and Benediction and other liturgical forms proper to the congregation should be the meat of our reflections. Already some communities are using, as the Church intends, appropriate parts of the Divine Office for morning and evening prayers. The examination of conscience is inserted into Compline. The monks of the Middle Ages were often unlettered and could not read, but ruminated on the breviary's biography of a saint or the Introit of the Mass and so on. There were few books anyway, since they had to be copied by hand. Very important and frequently forgotten is the fact that long passages of the Bible were committed to memory. Only a hundred years ago some orders placed the burden of memorizing the entire psalter, before being admitted to profession, upon their novices. Besides the common custom in past ages of memorizing the Rule, the frequency of certain Epistles and Gospels at Mass contributed to a storehouse of passages for meditation. I do not advocate a return to memorizing, since books are so available nowadays, but I do believe our official prayers must begin for more of us to express our inner sentiments and resolutions as they are garnered the livelong day.

The next chapters will touch upon the Mass as the focus of the day and upon the difficulties of practicing mental prayer. It is so easy to leave the chapel in the morning after Mass and the prayers with which we surround the Mass, thinking on our way to breakfast, "Well, that's over for today!" As I said above, Christ is with us during the Mass, but abides with us with the power of his grace all day. We put on Christ, as St. Paul tells us, but Christ equally puts on us, acts through us, the members of his Mystical Body. The Christ-likeness, which was sketched upon us at baptism, outlined more clearly with each new sacrament and colored vividly by our profession of vows, must be given details and shading and tints and hues by a daily closer conformity to Christ. It is from the liturgy that we learn the virtues we should practice all day long. Much of this learning is, of course, unconscious, but not the less effective if it informs our mind and conditions our will.

We cannot think of the celebration of the Mass and the Divine Office as merely our human gift to the Father through Christ. The whole liturgy is inter-action. We proclaim our desire to live in charity and justice with those who receive the Eucharist alongside us. Most important of all, Christ causes grace in us, as was explained in the early chapter on the life of the Trinity and the image of Christ in us. By our participation with *spirit* in liturgical prayers we who are vessels of grace also are vessels of election. Every baptized person shares in the priesthood as a cell in the Mystical Body, which offers the Mass in the person of the ordained priest at the altar. Whereas a Catholic without ordination cannot consecrate, he can *offer* by a share in the official prayers; he can *integrate* himself into the sacrifice by Holy Communion. Mystically and by their positive intention, finally, the Catholics who place themselves in union with the priest at the altar can be said to place their fingers around the host also at the consecration.

19 : "We Proclaim the Death of the Lord . . ."

EVERY MASS proclaims the death of the Lord until he comes in glory to judge the world. Every Mass is Calvary re-enacted. Although every human act of Christ contributed to the redemption of our souls, his crucifixion was the supremely salvific act, because out of the side of Christ was born the Church, which came of age by the Holy Spirit on Pentecost. Hence the daily Mass of a religious congregation is the occasion of gathering a specific "liturgical community" around the cross of the altar to witness the mystical death of Christ and the rebirth of his Church. This means that the merits Christ won for all times on Calvary are distributed principally by our sharing fully in the liturgy. We are "baptized," as it were, in the blood of the Lamb and are renewed as members of the Church.

Just as the whole Church was born out of the side of Christ on Calvary, so each congregation at the Mass (or renewal of Calvary) is reborn in the collective sense, not merely as individuals. The parish renews its bonds of charity as a neighborhood, it manifests Christianity collectively by aiding the poor, by educating its children, by opposing the local sources of crime and so on. The religious group is reborn mystically, too, and manifests its bonds to each other and its collective commitment to God by its apostolates and its joint expression of the Christ-life among men. And, most obviously, because the Eucharist is also a personal integration with God, the Mass is the occasion of the individual's rebirth. Finally because the Mass proclaims the *death* of the Lord, its message to the individual and to the liturgical community is that "unless the seed dies, it does not bear fruit." Personally and collectively we are called to sacrifice more than any lay person, because we claim through our profession a greater conformity to Christ.

It is important, in order to *worship* well and carry away the intended fruits of the Mass, to *believe* correctly. Perhaps the worst blows the Church has endured are from "devout" heretics who originally meant well. We have to understand the essence of the Sacrifice of the Mass so we can imitate what we witness and handle. It might be convenient to worship as we please, but it is an error to think we may approach God with whatever gift we find fitting without consulting him.

We are not bound by uniform externals, which are the spontaneous expression of every nation and century—whether an African drum or a Mexican guitar. Therefore the Protestants' earlier desire to use the vernacular is an external detail. But no one has the right to obviate the essentials demanded by God in his worship: "From the rising of the sun until it sets (all around the clock), to my name will be offered a clean (unbloody) sacrifice"—"This is my body and blood"—"Do this in memory of me." It is our obligation to find out the essential manner of worship that God decrees. We see these scriptural texts fulfilled in the Mass. This sacrifice is not just the courtesy God demands in approaching him—like a twenty-one gun salute for a head of state. The Mass is the vehicle by which God shares his life with us, hence he must decree how worship will be effected among us.

Wherever archaelogists dig into ancient civilizations and uncover the bones of the past, there seems to be evidence of religion and worship and especially sacrifice. Even prehistory records the continual urge of man to show fear of supernatural beings, reverence for the Lord of the universe, and dependence upon his providence for the sustenance of life. These sentiments are probably the relics of Paradise bolstered by our inborn faculty to reason to a provident Supervisor of the universe. In any event one can show no greater love for an ideal, reverence for divinity, or dependence upon a providence than by losing one's life in its cause. "No greater love has a man than he lay down his life." Therefore we eulogize the soldier who dies a patriot, the mother who dies for a child, the motorist who deflects his car from hitting a jaywalking pedestrian and so dies himself.

It is pointless and impossible to keep slashing one's wrists in order to express an act of religion. Nevertheless human sacrifice was most common among primitive nations and even within sophisticated cultures of the past, from Mesopotamia to Hawaii. Similarly the sacrifice of suicide is not an uncommon tradition. In the Vietnam War we read of Buddhist monks dousing themselves with gasoline and setting themselves aflame as a politico-religious protest. There arose, however, a subtler form of the sacrifice of life among civilized peoples—the offering of food, grain, oil, fruit and animal flesh. In effect the sacrificer says, "Look, God, I cannot keep dying to show my dependence upon you as the Giver of Life, but I would be willing to do so, if you required it. Instead I offer what *supports life*, these fruits of the field or trees and animals. As I destroy these supports of life (by killing or burning or the spilling of liquids, as wine), so do I symbolically sacrifice my life to you."

I do not for a moment believe the typical Roman or Hebrew customarily adverted to this fact, because a sacrifice to them was a propitiation or "bargain" with God, as it was popularly conceived. In the same way the people at Sunday Mass rarely conceive of the coins and bills as symbolic of what supports life because money provides shelter, clothes, food and warmth. Since religious cannot offer *things* at their Mass, one of their immediate and fruitful reflections on the Offertory (as the presentation of gifts to God) is that they must offer their voluntary service in the apostolate with the hosts and wine. Religious already belong to God completely. *They can only give him their future in a renewal of vows.* This is very appropriate because by their apostolate and religious profession they "make their living," humanly speaking, as a man punches a clock at the factory. And just as the "widow's mite" in the Gospel story exceeded the rich man's contribution, so that religious gives the most in his Offertory gift who strips himself of goods, pleasure and his own will most completely. I think, in order to underline the relationship between the Eucharistic sacrifice and religious profession, the ceremony of pronouncing or renewing vows should take place logically within the Mass at the Offertory.

If the Mass is to be an unbloody sacrifice, where is the destruction of food or life in the Mass? This is not as apparent as one might think. It is really the most important question one can pose about the Mass. What is the essence of sacrifice? Actually the theologians debated this centuries before it was settled by the words of Pope Pius XII. Some had previously maintained the sacrifice was Christ's humiliation under the appearance of a mere host and wine, his reduction to a "less worthy" state, or his consumption by men as the Sacred Species, a type of destruction. We attend so many Masses in our lives, that to understand fully and profit by them, we have to see how they are a re-enactment of Good Friday's history.

How did Christ die on the cross? After being scourged and bruised and crowned with thorns—causing already the loss of a considerable amount of blood—Christ was nailed to the cross. His weight was suspended from the nails in such a way that, whether or not he straddled a supporting stick, as some say, he had to heave himself upward from where his feet were fastened, in order to breathe. His lungs must have been agonizingly constricted by the pull in three directions from his body. To draw a free breath a crucified person had to summon every vestige of strength to lift his body and relax the tension upon his torso. Men who were tied to a cross, rather than fastened by nails, sometimes lingered for several days until exhaustion and weakness from lack of food asphyxiated them. Either because the two thieves were actually fastened by ropes, as often shown by artists, or had not lost so much blood prior to crucifixion, they were not near death as the sun fell and the Jewish holiday began. Therefore the legs of the two thieves were broken with clubs precisely so they could no longer force their bodies into the position necessary to draw a free breath. As soon as they died from lack of oxygen their bodies could be removed from the crosses, lest Jewish sensibilities be offended by the sight during the Passover and the passerby be made ritually unclean.

Christ seemed dead already, so the centurion merely pierced his side to open the heart. From it flowed the few drops of blood remaining and the serous fluid, or "water." Hence we say Christ died from *shedding all his blood* rather than from asphyxiation. This is a rather critical point in the light of Pope Pius' words identifying the essence of the Mass. Christ is once more—mystically or mysteriously or sacramentally—placed in the state of a victim executed on the cross exactly when, at the Consecration of the Mass, his Body and Blood are separated. There is no suffering in the Mass, of course, and the Species' represent to us the living Body and Blood of Christ. Hence one receives the whole Christ in the Eucharist even under one form. But the Council has restored communion under both forms for special occasions to emphasize that the essence of the Mass is the separate consecrations of the Species. Dogmatists even point out that there would be no true Mass if a priest deliberately consecrated under only one Species. Whether Mass is celebrated in a Chinese pagoda, a shack in the jungle or aboard a submarine at the North Pole, the graces of Good Friday are being communicated to the "little churches" being born anew, perhaps only as a transitory congregation, out of the side of the mystically crucified Christ.

A religious whose spiritual life is sparked by the Mass (and the liturgy of the Divine Office and other prayers surrounding the Mass) should find every means—reflection, the use of the missal, participation—to focus his mind on this central point of the Mass. Liturgists decry the use of the rosary or "devotional" prayerbooks during Mass because they hinder us from offering the Mass in union with the priest, prevent us from savoring the particular spiritual food in the changing Propers of the Mass and make us less aware of the renewal of Calvary specifically at the twofold consecration.

When we bring up the subject of Holy Communion as *integrating* us with the sacrifice, it is useful to look again through the centuries. When the ancient peoples burned their flour cakes, spilled a libation of wine from their cups or slew their sacrificial animals, they characteristically ate or drank a portion of the sacrifice. Whether they were conscious of identifying or integrating themselves with the destroyed victims is not clear in every case. In effect they were saying, "Look, God, I am identifying myself with the sacrifice I have offered so that the unity even better expresses my dependence upon you for life and my willingness to die as the sacrifice itself was destroyed!" This mystique of prayer, whether instinctive or intentional, is the perfect introduction of pre-Christian mankind to the Eucharist. St. Augustine boldly asserted that everything good in pagan life—Greek philosophy or the universal *pax Romana* at the time of Christ's birth—is the *praeparatio evangelica,* "preparing for the Gospel."

The Eucharist, both in the temporary possession of Christ in the Communion of the Mass and in the abiding presence of Christ on the altar of reservation, is a divine "plot" to steal our heart, a happy measure to signify Emmanuel—"God with us." Without the reception of the Eucharist the Mass lacks the wholeness of sacrifice and identification, which is the sign of our conformity with Christ. If God had not said it, who could believe it? St. Bernard actually says we become gods for a moment! And why not, since God has become man for us?

As the religious community collectively offers its service implicitly during Mass when it delivers the Offertory gifts and is collectively reborn by its repeated "baptism" in the Blood of Christ during Mass, so the collective community is more strongly linked within its own membership by the reception of the Eucharistic Christ among them. The Fathers of the Church appreciated this bond of charity in their allusions to the physical constitution of the host and wine. As the grains of wheat must be plucked and crushed and ground and refined of their impurities collectively, the individuals must be snatched from merely natural life, then surrender their own identities and purposes to receive a collective identity as the Mystical Body of Christ. As the individual grapes are pressed and made to yield their precious liquor and become part of their new existence as wine, so the members of the community yield their persons to Christ. The community puts on Christ as Christ puts on the community: as the hosts and wine are signs of Christ's Eucharistic presence, so the religious are signs of Christ analogously "incarnated" again in their persons. The theological links between the dogmas of the Eucharist and the life of the Trinity (or grace within us) mutually reinforce each truth. Even though the dogmas are both profound and unexplainable mysteries, they are not difficult in the plain statement of their content and meaning to us religious.

The title of this chapter indicates that the Mass (and our living by its fruits) proclaims the death of the Lord *until he comes.* As I mentioned in an earlier chapter, religious are the visible symbol of hope that a mortified and dedicated life is worthwhile because of the glory of the resurrection. A subtle theologian might speculate at this point on the eternal Mass and Communion with Christ after the final judgment. As the death of Christ is renewed in the Mass, so the resurrection of Christ will have its parallel in our own glorification. The only point I wish to emphasize here is that the Eucharist is the very basis of our hope. In one feast it is called "the pledge of future glory." An adequate appreciation of the Mass does not stop with Good Friday; it looks to Easter. As our bodies and souls were more often sanctified temples of the indwelling Trinity on earth, so much greater is our guarantee of glory in heaven. The proportion of glory—which is the intensity of earth-won grace transfiguring us in heaven—is the degree of Eucharistic conformity we have known on earth. Sister is correct in the homely metaphor she uses with the third grade: everyone is a hundred per cent happy in heaven, but the capacity of each varies from a thimble to a box car.

How would I express the eschatology of the Mass and Eucharist? Everyone who reaches heaven possesses the Beatifying Vision of the Trinity, if only from a keyhole vantage point. But those who are most conformed to Christ will enjoy the Blessed Trinity with the gates of Paradise flung wide open and with the knowledge and love of God in panavision, technicolor and cinerama!

20 : The Prayer of Contact

You rise in the morning, make a hasty sign of the cross or a familiar morning offering, wash and dress and reach the chapel just on time. You mouth the customary prayers and preparation for Mass. You page through the Missal and observe every rubric. After reading or repeating your favorite thanksgiving the morning cycle is over. Sometimes between waking and breakfast you or someone else may have read the points of a meditation through which you struggled bravely to concentrate. During this whole morning process you may actually never have prayed, that is, lifted your mind and will and emotions to make contact with God. What you have done is prepare yourself for contact. Thousands of vocal prayers, including Mass and Holy Communion, do not necessarily add up to one contact.

At eleven o'clock in the morning when you glance at a crucifix, you may say, "You did it for me, Christ." At eleven-thirty, when you are irritated, you may say, "Lord, help me to keep quiet like you did." At noon when you pass the chapel, you may say, "Hello, Lord; thanks for yourself in Holy Communion today and every day of my life." Your prayer-life began at eleven in the morning, if that is the first time you *encountered* God during your day.

Is there no merit in the early-morning prayer cycle? Like everything any Christian does in the state of grace, in the concrete it adds up for heaven or for hell, that is, glory or expiation, at least in purgatory. If actions are performed consciously out of duty and a sense of virtue, it pleases God the more. If there is present at least a virtual intention of union with and imitation of Christ, our actions come closer to the nature of prayer, which is contact. The Apostle urges us to do all things in the name of Christ, whether we eat or drink or sleep or work. It is in this sense that work is prayer. But prayer, as we commonly understand it, is awareness of a Person, who is attentive to us in return. Generally you are talking to Someone who is listening, or else you listen to him for light and inspiration—in the sense of a growing conviction to improve your life or receiving an insight into Scriptures or religious life you never had before. Words are not necessary for contacts; sometimes, as we shall see, words impede contact.

What of the routine "endurance" of Mass and the Divine Office? Is there merit or self-improvement without contact? "These people praise me with their lips, but their heart is far from me," God complained in the Old Testament. Hence vocal prayer is profitable to the soul to the degree in which it mirrors the sentiments of the soul. When the Rule or law of the Church itself requires us to pray, at least there is the merit of obedience of a task properly executed. But that is too little. Even if one does not advert to the meaning of the specific words, as when they are in Latin, the general meaning of the feast or liturgical action need not escape us: The Good Shepherd, the place of Mary at the feast at Cana, the essence of the Mass at the Consecration, the availability of Christ in the Eucharist during Benediction. Hence *recollection and aspirations of a general nature is the minimal contact we should have with God during any prayer*—or during our entire workday, for that matter.

But the optimal contact we strive for is to understand and realize the meanings of the vocal prayers we say during the liturgy or privately. If we are reading the *Ordo*, shuffling holy cards, and unbraiding ribbons as we say, "O God, incline to my aid and make haste to help me," it does not ring true. Many Catholics, including religious, would be singularly struck by the "Our Father," if they realized they were asking God to forgive them *to the degree* in which they forgive their debtors; their lips praise, but their heart is not intent on the meaning of the words. Some religious make certain phrases of the Mass or Divine Office points of contact with God—perhaps the "Glory be" at the end of each psalm recalling the indwelling Trinity within them. Prayer is a personal endeavor and hard work, when the novelty wears off and we face years and years of driving ourselves to recollection and meditation and vocal prayers. Each religious must attempt to condition his soul with the techniques that work best—like the "points of return" at the "Glory be." Some of us will never be able to think of the meaning of each verse during the length of a single psalm, even at the end of our lives. But this should be no cause for concern *if we maintain a parallel level of awareness of God's presence* as we recite psalms and orations. This means we have a sense of well-being that God is praised, that we are doing our duty, that the image of Christ is being clarified in our souls through grace, that we are receiving new insights into Catholic doctrine from the fragments of prayer that do reach our conscious level of thinking.

I suspect many religious would be overjoyed if this last paragraph *could* apply to their vocal prayer-life. Once more it is a question of natural conditioning aiding grace and not simply expecting the grace of God to supply a satisfactory prayer-life without our conscious exertion. An analogy to this conditioned recollection which is parallel to the somewhat mechanical recitation of a prayer, is the Rosary. We strive to keep a mental image of the mystery announced when we say the vocal prayers, as it is unlikely that most of us can energize some fifty "Hail Mary's" in any other way. The repetitious prayers tend otherwise to lose their significance. Some religious can maintain the "parallel recollection" by keeping before them a holy card or statue or crucifix that happens to appeal to them. They can be changed or discarded according to one's spiritual need. This reliance upon images (or liturgical colors, vestments, art forms, and all sacramentals) is appropriate and consonant with human nature and the spirit of the liturgy. Unfortunately out of human respect—the desire not to appear externally more devout than our co-religious—we often disregard useful means of reinforcing the meanings of the prayers we recite.

How shall we answer those who say nothing works for them at prayer? First of all, serious sin and a meaningful prayer-life cannot peacefully co-exist. I will pass over any further comment because each person must judge himself. In order to suggest some remedies and explain some of the difficulties of prayer, I will make some general comments, which will be relevant mostly to mental prayer.

Regardless of failure to pray well—assuming it is actually a failure—one cannot abandon prayer, by which I mean the desire to know God by direct contact, whether during public or private prayer. St. Teresa of Avila, whose "castles of perfection" outline all of prayer-life, was no stranger to difficulties in prayer. During an early period of lukewarmness she neglected prayer for some time and forced herself to pray again; Our Lord subsequently revealed during one of their chats that she would have lost her soul if she had not returned to prayer! Yet you can scarcely open a book about prayer without reading that she passed eighteen years without receiving a single comfort or delight in it. But she doggedly persevered and became the saint she is. St. Vincent de Paul experienced only two years of dryness at prayer, but the aridity was accompanied by terrifying temptations against his faith in God and the Eucharist. He sewed the word, *Credo,* "I believe," over his heart inside his cassock and touched it when he could not muster the affections to resist temptation strongly. The point I am making about not abandoning the exertion of prayer is that we cannot dictate to God about the graces we desire. We may not set a limit on how long we shall endure. We may not use our loyalty to God as a bargaining point.

St. Francis de Sales discouraged too much introspection and dissection of one's prayer-life. He wrote, "Whoever prays fervently does not know if he prays well or not, for he does not think of the prayer he says, but of God to whom he says it." Although it is true one ought not to dissect his own life too picayunely, it is certainly an asset to know the broad directions of most religious' prayer-life. It is not necessary here to review distinctions or multiply subdivisions and opinions.

In general we can isolate three levels of mental prayer. (I am using "mental prayer" to include those contacts with God during which we use our own faculties and resources instead of someone else's words.) The first level of mental prayer emphasizes our *reason*. Perhaps we start off with a point suggested by a meditation book. Then we amplify the scene recalled from our Lord's life, for example, or apply some point of the Rule and Constitutions to our personal lives. The second level of mental prayer, towards which the reasoning has impelled us, is *aspiration* or *affection*. Often the meditation book supplies some phrases appropriate to the "point" proposed. The important point is to pray in our own words. In fact, if we were able to skip the reasoned part of mental prayer and spend a whole half-hour in pouring out sentiments of love, it would be profitable to close our minds to any reasoning at all, because it is better to talk to God than *about* him. Most of us could not sustain a half-hour daily of such an outpouring of emotional prayer. An equal part of this second level of mental prayer is making *good resolutions and determinations of our will* to do something concretely, especially that day, to grow in grace. We will try to speak kindly to someone who daily irritates us. We will sequester our thoughts better during the Divine Office by disposing ourselves beforehand. As is obvious, these acts of the will are couched in somewhat emotional language. Hence it is an easy transition to the next stage of mental prayer. The third level has been called by several names, particularly the prayer of *simplicity* or even *contemplation*. This is not that contemplation which God alone can infuse by enfolding the soul within himself. That simplicity or contemplation to which I refer is acquired by our own efforts, assisted by grace. No Christian is barred from acquiring this third level of mental prayer. St. Bonaventure teaches it is the natural heritage of everyone who chooses to attain it. This is what I prefer to call the *prayer of serenity*, when our faculties are calm, reasoning is silenced, the will merely longs for union with God and conformity to Christ without specific acts, the motions and sentiments are generalized into a feeling of being caught up into the divine life. I believe every religious who tries to pray well experiences this feeling periodically, even though it may be of only a few minutes' duration.

It was necessary to isolate these forms of mental prayer in order to explain some of the difficulties we experience. I look upon these levels as very fluid. We pass from one to the other without being aware of it. Nor should we try to be aware of it. Too many religious consciously try to force themselves into a higher level, because it supports their ego to imagine the great progress they are making. If an outpouring of emotions occurs, it should be released. If the soul relaxes into the vivid serenity of the awareness of God, it should not be forced to reason. If serenity and affections are both lost, the mind must be stirred by reasoning before the religious falls asleep or wanders into distraction. It requires humility and emotional maturity—self-knowledge in the best sense—to accept ourselves as we are in our prayer-life.

A simple rule is to be *serene* when it is easy to concentrate on the tabernacle or crucifix or some image without our faculties operative; to pour out an *act of the will and emotions* if it finds easy expression; but to return to our reading when we are physically tired or very distracted. It is a mistake to limit reading, in fact, to a few sentences and stop, if no aspirations are forthcoming. It is even bet-

ter to *read slowly and thoughtfully* a whole half-hour
rather than be frustrated by distractions and sleep. If the
points are read from a common meditation book, the religious should procure supplemental reading as necessary
and use it without embarrassment. Once more merely external forms must surrender to the needs of souls. In the
earlier period of monasticism there was no formal meditation, but spiritual reading at a deliberate and thoughtful pace fused with mental prayer. In the case of a religious who finds a particular time of the day more apt for
mental prayer, he should exchange the times of spiritual
reading or possibly some other daily activity with meditation. Many of us are not persuaded by an author's flights
of fancy or poetic, sentimental treatises on love and ab-
negation. Authors of meditation books should be forced
to write them from five to six o'clock in the morning, so
that they can use the same materials to keep us alert
which have succeeded with them. Even those who are
wakeful may not be as imaginative as the author. Let
everyone seek a meditation book written in his own key.
Let that book be one which fosters contact with God. It
is possible to meditate, which is the use of reason, without making mental prayer, which is conversation. The
"reasoning" during meditation is not an end in itself.

The physical inability to remain aware, regardless of
the meditation book or the time of day or the position of
body we adopt, is also emotionally exhausting because of
our frustration. We need a great deal of patience, even if
we foresee a lifetime of such frustration. If sleep and distractions overwhelm us despite our efforts, there is no loss
of grace, but conversely I doubt if there is much spiritual
progress, since one must be awake and alert to speak
with and listen to God. We shall have to pay attention if

it takes dousing our face with ice water or running around the house to get some oxygen to the brain. However, there is a simple expedient possible to all. I advise the religious to choose any time of the day he wishes and spend *just ten alert minutes* in aspirations or in serenity. Ten minutes of *real contact*, perhaps directly after Mass, will compensate for the *sincere* but inept half-hour of frustration.

Sometimes the best conversation with God during mental prayer is precisely about the distractions themselves, since they seem to be so important to us. "Lord," you might say, "I've got to attend that boring meeting today. Help me to find time to get my notes in order and sit through it patiently." Or, "I'm looking forward to my vacation, God. I'll enjoy seeing my family and traveling. But let it be the occasion of charitable conversation and real relaxation, not just a mad rush from place to place." Or, "I'm sorry I squelched my co-religious yesterday. It's getting so I hate to look at him (her) when I pass. Help me force myself to be polite and act as if nothing happened yesterday."

Too much has been said in spiritual books about aridity in prayer, as if it were a symbol of the advanced, but "patiently suffering" religious. We ought not exaggerate our "dark night of the soul." So much supposed aridity is merely the lack of effort. To qualify for the "dark night," one should simultaneously be suffering terrible frustrations or intolerable physical pain or persecution by his co-religious or helplessness in the face of the need of those he loves. This is not the same as that aridity in prayer which can be frequently remedied by "shifting gear" into another level of prayer. Nor should one call the absence of sweetness or elation in prayer, so common in early religious life, true aridity. Consolation is what God gives us, not what we give God, which is the essence of virtue. In fact, much of what passes as the "gift of God" in the early consolatory stages of prayer is just a *natural* uplifting due to the novelty of our life or our sentimental sighing over being a special ward of God's providence. But grace can build on this natural attraction.

Later on, if true aridity develops—not just the kind due to inept practices of mental prayer—God will also supply the graces of perseverance. In heaven God will compensate for the disgust and weariness we experience on earth. There is no other solution than to wait patiently for the visitation of God, even rejoicing at the invitation to live in dark faith and without comfort. One can only go to the simplest form of prayer, a sigh, a glance at the Crucified. The mystics tell us that the highest level of prayer is not founded on any activity of our own, and looks directly to God the Father conceived in a totally spiritual way. At such a time a soul is lifted even beyond the Humanity of Christ and all concrete images. A true spiritual aridity might be a preparation for just that. This is the reason for mystics writing that they cannot explain such a contact with God in human terms; there is simply no basis of comparison without concrete images. The point is that we should not be concerned about these specialized contacts with God. We cannot prepare for them, but we should always be ready to turn a corner and bump into God without being surprised.

21 : By Way of Summary

So MUCH of this book has been written under the prompting of others and with their ideas and problems in mind, that no small part of it should be in quotation marks. Yet so many areas have not been touched. The place of Mary in the prayer-life of the religious, the Bible as the starting point of religious perfection, the saints as exemplars, the need of more "intellectualism" in understanding the vows and the religious state, neurosis in the religious life: these are only some of the topics that must be left for a second volume—God willing! In fact, we religious are so wrapped up in the more refined concepts of perfection, that we overlook the importance of just being a good Catholic and keeping our sense of awe for the mystical and divine. A whole series of chapters could explore the meaning of Christ's mysteries in our lives, for example, the Sacred Heart as the supreme expression of the importance of the emotions in public and private prayers.

Although I have used "order" in the sense of any religious institute, the distinctions in law and practice are manifold. Although I have used the masculine pronouns to designate also women religious, when I wrote in general terms, not everything was, of course, applicable to both sexes. Moreover, whether by nature or conditioning, women do not have the same specific problems in the religious life as men. Hence I was left with the feeling that I did not fully explore the religious life of women. Because the training of religious brothers ranges from the simple catechism to the doctorate, the relevance of everything I wrote about their status in the Church is open to question. But I will claim some success for myself if I at least opened issues and debate without solving anything by an *ipse-dixit.*

My chief concern was to interpret the religious life for the twentieth-century after thinking about it for eighteen years and asking questions. Centuries of accretion have to be separated from fundamental notions of perfection; the values of psychology and modern trends of politics and technology have to be analyzed to benefit the religious state. It is the failure to appreciate what is good in the world and in individual humans that weakens young vocations. Experiment, challenge, curiosity bespeak a search for meaningfulness, not an attempt to criticize. Hence I have written on the vows in the "sacramental" sense of giving us a new status in the Church with the duty and right of seeking significant ways to bear witness to the eternal truths of the Gospel. Vocational doubts rise from the order itself not providing the meaning, as well as from the member's exaggerated desire for absolute certainty of his call from God. But a vocation is God calling us through the agency of religious superiors. Once a candidate has made himself available by presenting himself to the order, he had better search his soul before leaving merely because of human disillusionment or simple laxity. The question is whether an individual can sanctify himself in the milieu of the order and can find satisfaction in its apostolates. The nature of a vocation is such that the backwardness of an order and the ignorance of its leaders are only indirectly relevant to a vocation: is the member such a weak creature of environment that he or she cannot achieve spiritual perfection within such an order and perhaps change its directions by example and dialogue? Faith in God's providence leads us to believe that he uses natural attractions and apparently coincidental events to lead us into a particular religious order.

Understandable is the first fervor of youth, which will wane in time. Spiritual directors should help young religious distinguish between initial uplift and the enduring meaning of prayer. The young must accept themselves for what they are in God's eyes, with defects of personality and many sins, and start into religious life as a *school* of perfection. They must see the aphorisms of the saints as representing the ideal or mature or formed religious, whose virtue and prayer-life are the *culmination* and final stages of the sincere following of Christ. Therefore the decisions based on discouragement or elation or any emotional excess are unfounded in reality. One must keep acting for a long time *as if* he had the requisite virtue and personality, in order to decide maturely and objectively. Nor does one set a timetable for the Holy Spirit's operations.

The meaning of religious life has become more externally individual than ever before. Each one has to decide how his personality and talents can be used more effectively under the dominion of his superiors. The instinct for poverty and the conviction of obedience, however, cannot be legislated. Never before have religious had such an opportunity to baptize the world's products and technology and even insights into humanity itself. We stand within the world's pattern of life without the appearance of smug superiority and implied derogation, but with the conviction that faith and human knowledge complement each other and do not merely co-exist uneasily.

But of all those in the world we serve and of all those to whom we are sent as missionaries, we bear witness to the Christ-life most of all to our own co-religious. Charity is the seal of the holy person, impressing him with *apostolic* virtue for the most important area of its expression, the monastery, the friary, the convent. The social meaning of charity is our awareness of the failings of others without reflexive commentary—that is, we cannot be unconscious of another's obvious defects, but we can condition ourselves to stop setting a moral value on the other person's actions. It is the nature of the human mind to see virtue or vice implicitly in another's acts, but no one can sin until he has "commented," at least in his own mind. This aspect of uncharitableness and rash judgment is not clear in the minds of untrained religious.

The truism that grace builds on nature, therefore, is receiving new emphasis in the current training of the young. Spontaneous enthusiasm must be channelized, not thwarted as the expression of some "lower" instinct. As the religious begins to love himself properly, he will begin to love the world to which he has been sent. He begins inside the religious house with the example of unaffected holiness, companionship, community loyalty, ready availability to assist others, and spiritual friendship. No one relates sincerely to laymen in one's apostolate unless he first accepts those among whom God has placed him immediately. This does not mean that one begins the religious life being able to like everyone else about him, but it does mean that gradually the members almost casually accept each other as they are.

The restoration of Paradise, I said, will never be complete until the moral rectitude Adam lost is regained by willingness to serve each other. The superior must teach and "walk with men" as God did in the Garden, that is, place himself on the same level without surrendering his dignity or final authority. The subject must respond to this love of service by keeping the vow. In neither case is their service to each other to be made dependent upon the other's fulfillment of his part, however, for our service is primarily to God himself. It is not that the meaning of obedience in modern life is on the wane, but that the significance of individual endeavor is on the increase. "Blind" obedience is still valid in the sense of not judging the superior's reasons, and obeying even when the reasons are not clear, although the subject should be allowed, or rather encouraged to bring the light of his experience or technical knowledge to bear upon the superior's decisions.

In poverty particularly must the individual and the order give witness to the *baptized uses of the world*. Of all the virtues associated with religious life, poverty above all must be assessed in the context of the environment wherein it is to be practiced, not by other nations or centuries. Poverty is not merely the absence of possession, but the putting on of Christ also externally. Chastity is likewise not merely the absence of some human in our lives, but an affirmation of the value of making God the "other half of our souls," the complement of our personality. Without prayerful experience of Christ's intimacy in his life, the religious succumbs easily to lesser influ-

ences, just as not putting on Christ by means of the sim-
plification that poverty gives to us causes a religious to
possess and to desire to possess the earth instead of the
Creator.

Both poverty and chastity have counterfeits in false
puritanism. Human drives are all good, particularly in
view of Christ's motivation in becoming a human,
whether Adam sinned or not. However, to restore inbal-
ance in our drives (as they manifest themselves in our
sins), mortification should primarily consist of disciplin-
ing and denying those excessive "passions" which cause
us trouble to master, rather than crossing nature all of the
time for its own sake. This is what I called the "mortification of atonement." The "mortification of the present moment" refers to the discipline imposed by unsought frustrations and the daily onus of religious life and the apostolate. No one should presume to multiply mortifications
or prayers indiscriminately, until what is required by the
horarium is faithfully pursued.

Precisely because every member is unique, no one can
judge (and only the competent can advise) what is individually appropriate. No one type of personality has a
monopoly on heaven. This is the great value for us in
reading the lives of the saints. No one should be forced to
warp himself as a religious, although what is offensive to
the community or laity must be corrected. Otherwise the
person may be unfit for the religious state. Although a
member should take first vows without reservation and
without simply delaying his final choice of God until perpetual vows, the time of temporary vows is a safety valve
for the superiors in discerning the fit. Above all, superior
or subject, every member's personality must be assessed
apart from his moral character. The emotional forces in

one's life, especially, have to be directed into purposeful apostolates and personal growth, because emotions are an expression of the *whole* person.

Our sins and pretensions will gradually give ground if we humbly wait for God's supporting grace, while we simultaneously act as if growth in holiness depended upon our enthusiasm alone. Often we have to simulate the externals of religious life, when we seem only failures to ourselves. This is not evil, because deception is not our purpose; we are rather trying to condition ourselves externally to engender interior forces. The long-range goals of ultimate victory and self-conquest and intimacy with Christ are the most important signs of the emotionally mature religious, who still can fail in virtue, of course.

Besides the individual, an equal concern of the religious state is the community as an *organization*. Of the activities in which the members conjointly engage, worship is the chief endeavor, not the apostolate, which is rather the result of worship. Our official prayers are the spawning ground of private prayers all day long. Yet Mass and the Office would be spiritual food enough, if we could align our thoughts and sentiments to reflect the Church-at-prayer. Liturgy is the matrix of the day-long sanctifying process. The Mass repeats the most important of Christ's redemptive acts, and Holy Communion integrates us both physically and mentally to the imitation of that sacrifice. But whenever the religious prays in a group or with written formulas, there is a danger of losing contact and spontaneity with God. Hence to *talk* with God as a responsive Person is the goal of mental prayer. Our words and mental operations may fail to support this conversation—yet our mental faculties are alert. We simply rest in the knowledge of God's presence in and about us. Extended through the day, this simple prayer of serenity becomes the spirit of recollection. It is beginning on earth the indescribable contact with the Trinity in heaven.

Every age must attempt to seek God in its own way, but within the framework of the Church's evolution of doctrine. Far from thinking we have become less intense as religious, it seems to me that each succeeding age should become a fuller, if different, expression of the proliferation of the Mystical Body at work and prayer. Perhaps our faith is not keen enough to discern this truth. But the vitality of each century should come from reinterpreting the Gospel and re-thinking its message. The "infant fervor" of the aspostolic Church was quite "free" and inspired. The bishops of the Second Vatican Council urged a return to the "charismatic" Church, when religion was less stylized, yet impelled countless martyrs to die gladly as a matter of course, if that was to be the consequence of their living the Gospel. Similarly we religious have to recover the pristine urgency of our founders without hedging and glosses. Christ was not an impractical dreamer. When St. Francis wished to live the evangelical life, the Pope thought it unrealistic, but the saint countered by asking if Christ would have commanded the impossible. We need this fundamentalist faith in our calling. We need to chip away the façade of piety that is irrelevant to twentieth-century religious, because the "letter of the law kills, but the spirit gives life."